WHITBY YARDS
THROUGH TIME
Alan Whitworth

AMBERLEY PUBLISHING

Dedicated to Bob and Judy Oldale –
True Friends and Lovers of Whitby

First published 2012

Amberley Publishing
The Hill, Stroud
Gloucestershire, GL5 4EP

www.amberley-books.com

Copyright © Alan Whitworth, 2012

The right of Alan Whitworth to be identified as the
Author of this work has been asserted in accordance
with the Copyrights, Designs and Patents Act 1988.

ISBN 978 1 84868 605 2

All rights reserved. No part of this book may be
reprinted or reproduced or utilised in any form
or by any electronic, mechanical or other means,
now known or hereafter invented, including
photocopying and recording, or in any information
storage or retrieval system, without the permission
in writing from the Publishers.

British Library Cataloguing in Publication Data.
A catalogue record for this book is available from
the British Library.

Typeset in 9.5pt on 12pt Celeste.
Typesetting by Amberley Publishing.
Printed in the UK.

Introduction

To visit Whitby's 'Yards' is to step back in time. Hardly changed from the Middle Ages, this is where one can still meet old Whitby – a secret Whitby – unspoilt and untroubled by the holiday visitor. The yards, alleyways and ghauts are some of my favourite places to explore. Though often private, there are however, so many surviving that are semi-public or public, insomuch as they are short-cuts from one street to another, that it is still possible to catch a glimpse of what this small seaport must have been like two or three hundred years ago.

Today, over eighty named yards still exist out of more than one hundred and there are, in addition, another thirty or so places of similar character but perhaps called 'steps', 'lane', 'square' or 'place'. The origins of the yards lay in the days of medieval Whitby and its development. At that period, the first parcels of land created and sold off or leased by the lord of the manor were formed of long narrow strips known as *burgages*, with a narrow side fronting onto the main street. This arrangement is particularly noticeable on the East Side along Church Street. The main house was then erected facing onto the highway, with the long garden or garth stretched out behind. Through successive generations, the garden was developed, perhaps firstly by sons eager to raise money from a new inheritance who then sold off a plot of land for building, usually at the furthest end of the garden away from the family home. Later, as more land was sold to raise revenue, more and more building took place, infilling from the back toward the main house. As a consequence of this development, access was obviously required to the properties behind the main residence and so a right of way was created alongside the main house from the highway down to the last property. In time, these became the well-loved yards and alleyways that are such a feature of the Whitby townscape.

Through the centuries, however, many of the yards have changed names; others, of course, have become lost through demolition and town redevelopment, a process still occurring even into the twenty-first century.

Today a walk up and down the yards often reveal well-kept and well-manicured areas, however, it should be remembered that in years gone by, these pockets of Whitby were perhaps some of the dirtiest and dingiest of the town.

Riddled with filth and poor sanitation, the yards were often over crowded with as many as thirty or forty families living in abject poverty. In 1816, 126 people lived in the now demolished 'America Yard', off Baxtergate. Eighty-six were crowded into the smaller Post Office Yard off St Ann's Staithe, an area known in medieval times as *Helle*. Concern about public health in the yards led to an annual inspection of all yards by the town's Medical Officer of Health (MOH). This later led to the demolition of numerous buildings because of the appalling condition of many of the properties and the lack of facilities.

Other byways to explore are Pier Lane; an ascent up the 'Donkey Road' beside the 199 Steps (Chair Stairs, once locally known as Jacob's Ladder), which should be properly named Church Lane and formerly known as Abbey Church Lane; and the descent on to the Cragg via the tunnel off Khyber Pass, which frames a spectacular and much-photographed view of Whitby Abbey.

Lastly, in 1995, Whitby gained an addition to the extensive heritage of ghauts and lanes. From Greens Yard, near the junction of Bridge Street and Church Street, a flight of sixty-five stone steps was built. Named 'Caedmon's Trod' after Whitby's famous cowman poet, these are another route to the abbey other than the 199 Steps. Well worth the climb, this new ascent offers a fresh vantage from which to appraise the town's endlessly fascinating townscape with its yards, lanes, steps and all. And finally, more recently, Bagdale Court has been created off Bagdale, behind what was the old Brewery site of Akenhead & Simpson. Here, the lovely eighteenth-century brewery house of red brick and stone quoins survives, along with the cobbles from the original staithes, which were from the days when Bagdale was an open and navigable waterway and boats would tie up to load and unload the barrels of beer and sacks of malts and such.

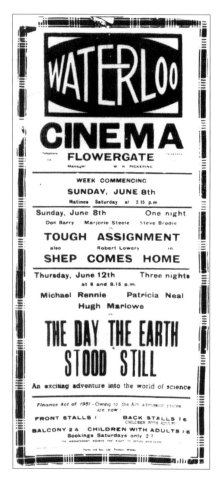

A film poster for the Waterloo Cinema, Waterloo Yard.

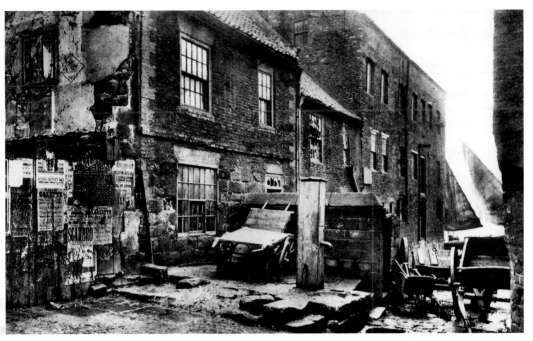

Alder's Waste Ghaut or Virgin Pump Yard

This took its name from the family of Henry Awder (or Alder), compass-maker, who had property here in 1644. Later it became known as Virgin Pump Ghaut. This is believed to be the site of Whitby's earliest Viking settlement. Near here was held the 'Thingwala' of Danish Whitby, the meeting-place where the courts of law-giving were held. Today, the 'Thingwala' survives and is perpetuated in the Isle of Man ceremony of similar name, 'Tynwald', (below). Both words originate from the Norse 'Thing' meaning 'to settle' (as in disputes). The whole area was demolished in April 1959, and the site is now the car park at the corner of Grape Lane and Church Street.

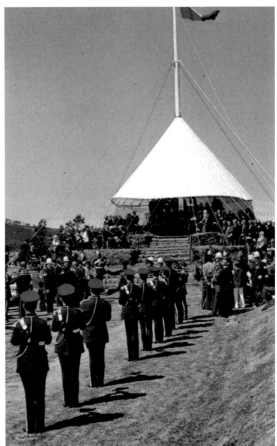

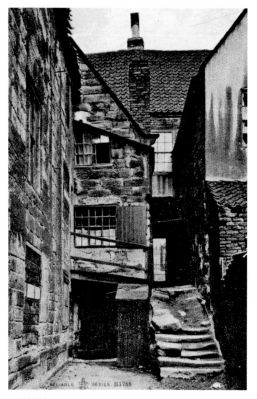

Arguments Yard *c.* 1895

At one period, there were two yards of the same title in Whitby from the family name Argument. The description following is that of the yard on the West Side and was made by the MOH (Ministry of Health) in 1896: 'Argument's Yard is one of the cobbled ones, and at the upper end it comes close to the cliff, and water – and sometimes dirt – washed down from the cliff side – gives the back of the houses a very dirty appearance. I told the tenants that they ought to keep it cleaner, but they told me that they had no sooner got it cleaned up than it was "lost in dirt" again. It is a great eye-sore, but I don't think that it does much harm. I had a complaint about one of the houses in this yard, but I found, on visiting it, that the complaint was unfounded.'

The yard off the Cragg was demolished 1956–60. The yard here is possibly one of the most well-known of all the yards and was popular with artists and photographers. Today the yard is a clean and neat place, the cottages mostly let out as holiday homes, but essentially little has changed over the years.

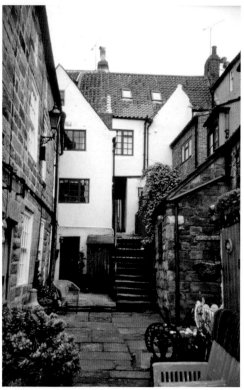

Arguments Yard, Church Street

The Reverend George Young in his work *A History of Whitby*, Vol. II, published in 1817, probably best describes the town at an early period when he wrote 'there was more propriety in calling the streets of Whitby at that era "gates", "gaites", or "ways", as they were very unlike the streets of the present day. When we speak of one of those ancient streets, we must not form in our minds the idea of a well-paved causeway, with a row of contiguous houses on either side; but figure to ourselves a kind of open, irregular road, scarcely paved at all, with the lands on both sides divided into tofts and half tofts, each containing one or more houses or cottages, with some space intervening, having a garden or garth behind, and perhaps a small garth in front. Such were the streets of Whitby for many ages after the time of the abbot Richard II; and while the streets were very irregular in their form, the houses were for the most part thatched cottages, constructed in the simplest manner, and bearing no resemblance to the elegant mansions of modern times...'

This view of Arguments Yard shows a group of locals carefully posed by the photographer as was often the custom in the nineteenth century when film exposures often took several minutes to achieve and so there were no 'candid' shots or moving photographs which can be so easily taken with modern cameras.

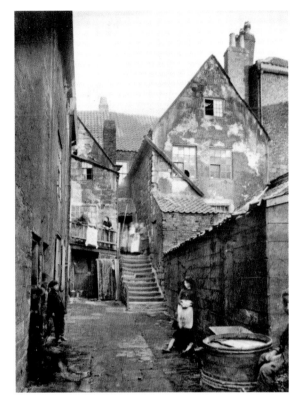

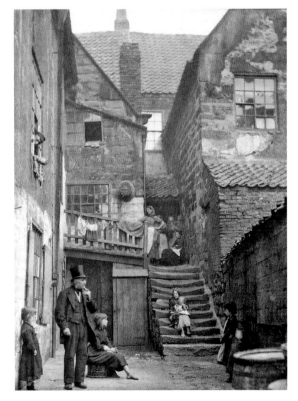

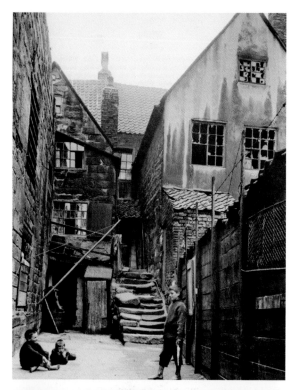

Arguments Yard *c.* 1913 & 1909

The Arguments Yard seen in these views off the cobbled end of Church Street, opposite the post office, also takes its title from a family of that name; and deeds of 1650 refer to Thomas Argment, with the same spelling occurring in 1830. In 1909 when the yard was painted by the artist A. Lister and appeared on this postcard (below), the MOH stated: 'In Argument's Yard there is now only one house that is inhabited, the rest of the property being left to its fate; but the owner has taken the precaution, which I wish others would follow, of nailing boards over the door and windows that can be reached, so that no one can get in.'

In 1899 John Knaggs, jet worker, lived at No. 1; at No. 2 was Mrs Eliza Noble; and at No. 3 resided Mrs Hannah Margaret Knaggs, who may or may not have been related to John at No. 1. In 1934, Arguments Yard was owned by Joseph Hicks, who lived at No. 6 and the dwellings – No. 1 to No. 5 – were occupied by twice as many as fifty years previous. By this date it is noticeable that the Knaggs family name no longer appears in this yard.

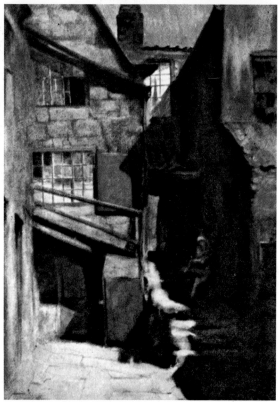

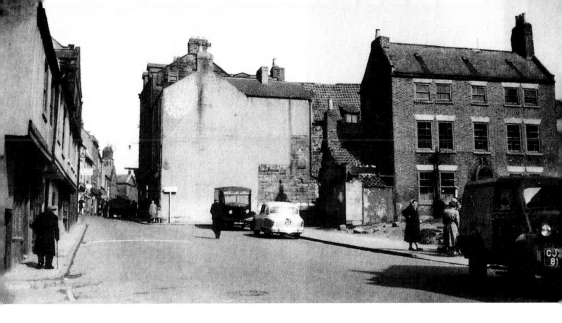

Ainsley's Court, off Church Street

The site of Ainsley's Court off Church Street was developed in the late-1950s. Demolition of many buildings hereabouts was necessary to widen Church Street. In 1899 a Mrs I. Ainsley lived at No. 1 Capella House. In 1909 it was said, 'Ainsley's Court is only a small yard; it is always kept in good repair'. Below, the same Tudor timber-framed jettied houses as seen in both photographs are some of the oldest property in Whitby. Whitby Abbey had a toll house hereabouts and a market, whose existence is retained in the local name for the bus stop as 'Tatie Market'.

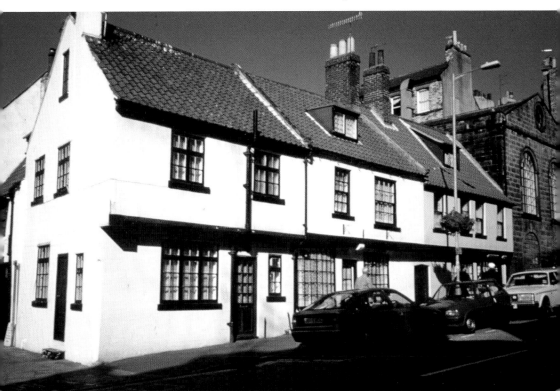

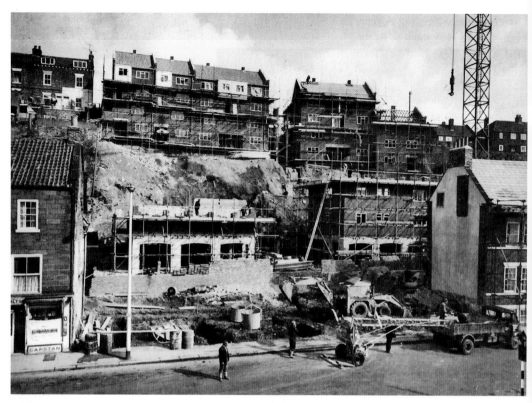

Ainsley's Court & Green's Yard off Church Street

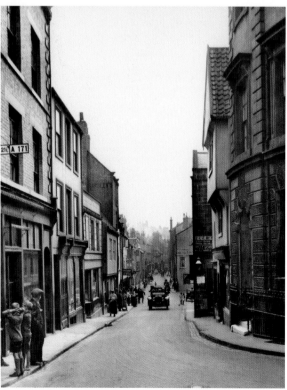

The site of Ainsley's Court and Green's Yard off Church Street was developed in the late-1950s. Demolition of many buildings hereabouts was necessary to widen Church Street, which from the photograph below taken in 1925, shows it was crucial. The motorcar is roughly in line with Ainsley's Court. In 1899 the residents included William Rymer, jet worker; John Philpot, sailor; and S. Dring a painter. By 1934 Capella House was uninhabited. Residents of Green's Yard in 1899 included a cabinet maker, labourer, riveter, groom, mariner and milk dealer.

Bolton's Yard (Demolished) & Bolton's Buildings, Flowergate

'In Bolton's Yard [off Church Street and now demolished], at the bottom, there is a stack of property that has tenements over a warehouse, and in these the following state of things exist: There is a small room with a bed in it, and a very small bed-place, for a man and his wife and two children. In the second there is a room with a bed in it and a small bed-place for a man, his wife, and three children. In the third there is a room with two bed-places in it, for a man, his wife, and four children. The whole is in bad repair, and there is only one privy for the whole lot. In addition, this privy is under the pantry of the second house. In the yard the channel is bad, and needs repair. I have recommended to the Council to serve the owner with a notice that these houses are unfit for human habitation.'

The principal owner in 1934 was Thomas Sayers Puckrin. Bolton's Buildings can be seen from Cliff Street and form part of McLacklin's Yard.

Bottom: In Gardiner's Yard off Flowergate, the MOH reported in 1909: 'Now in a fairly satisfactory condition; it is well-paved and is kept clean' – just as it is today.

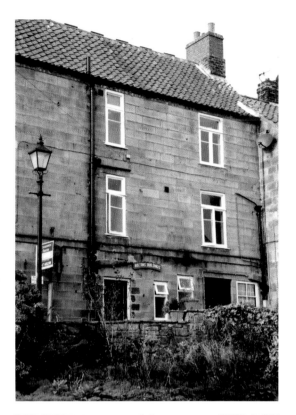

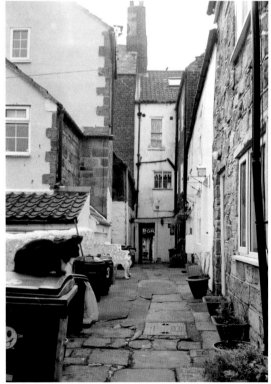

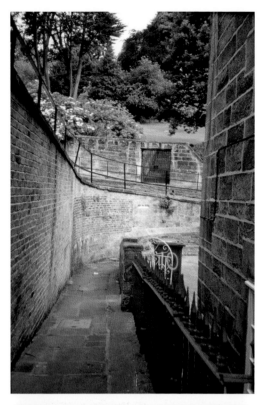

Bagdale Beck, Bridge and Carrs Yard

Bagdale Beck rises in Stakesby Vale and flows down into the harbour near the railway station. At its upper end it remains open, but from beyond the railway embankment, the waters are culverted under the road and still flow today. It was a navigable waterway up until the late nineteenth century. The raised 'causey' at the top end is a legacy of the days when it still flowed; as, indeed, is the dramatic change of levels to the houses below Broomfield Terrace, where a careful examination of the retaining brickwork shows that a bridge dated 1830 carried a small road over the open Bagdale Beck. In 1934 the owner was Jane Anne Rusdale. The Revd George Young in 1817 wrote: 'The streets, being then without pavement except at the sides, were worn deep and hollow; and the waste water, having no drains for its reception, formed a current in the midst, where it sometimes stagnated. In the winter season, the streets, especially at the entrances of the town, were scarcely passable; but, for the accommodation of the inhabitants, some of the principal streets had narrow walks, paved with flags, in front of the houses. These walks were most remarkable...the pavement was greatly elevated above the middle of the street, with steps descending from one part of the walk to another, and other steps, at different places, leading down to the street...'

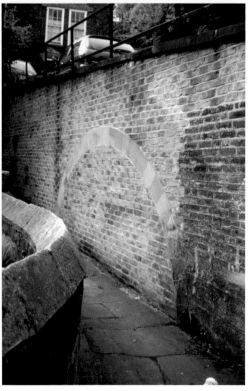

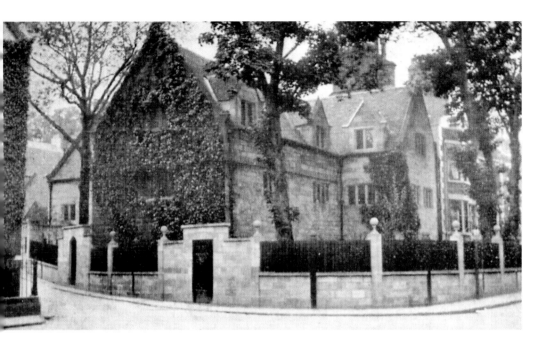

Bagdale Hall

Known as 'Backdale' in 1393, it begins at the foot of Chubb Hill. Bagdale Hall was originally erected *c.* 1515, but was heavily restored in the Victorian period and it is this façade that one sees today. When first built, it was described as 'nigh unto Whitby' and stood on the banks of Bagdale Beck and was surrounded by fields and orchards. It is known that the manorial court was held here, and witches were tried and then taken away and executed. Below, the modern day entrance to Bagdale Hall up Spring Hill which is part of the nineteenth-century addition to Bagdale Hall.

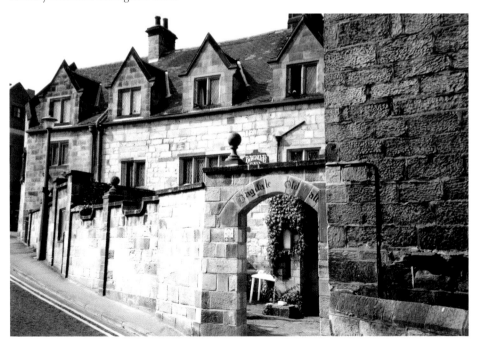

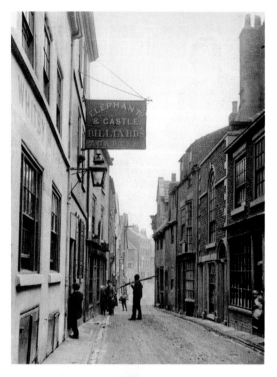

Bake House Yard off Haggersgate

James Russell Lowell, the famous American statesman, poet and man of letters wrote from Whitby to a friend in August 1887: 'I wish you could see the "yards" – steep flights of steps hurrying down from the West Cliff and the east, between which the river...crawls into the sea, and where I meet little girls with trays bearing the family pies to the baker...'

It was, of course, from the public bakehouse that Bakehouse Yard took its name. The bakehouse was a common institution in many towns and in Whitby there were at least nine. The reason for their existence was that the houses of poor folk had no ovens to bake bread and pies, so the ingredients were made up and then sent to the public bakehouse for cooking at the cost of a few pence. It was from this period that the tradition of adding decoration to pies came about, as it would be impossible to tell who each pie belonged to. The owner would therefore mark their pie with a suitable motif or pastry pattern. In the older picture, the young boy looking at the chimney sweep is turning into the entrance to Bakehouse Yard, next to the inn named The Elephant and Castle and today named The Star.

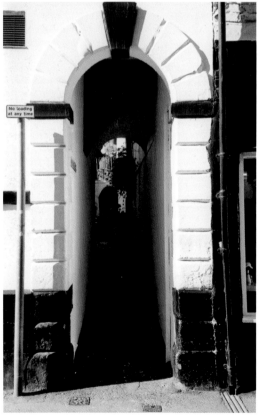

Henry Freeman (1835–1904)

Near the top of Bakehouse Yard is a house in which the famous Whitby lifeboat coxswain Henry Freeman lived; on the wall a plaque commemorates this fact. Henry was born the eighth child of William Freeman and his wife Margaret (neé Priestley) at Bridlington on 29 April 1835. His father was a brick-maker from the Vale of York and Henry at first took up this trade until about 1858 when he took to the sea, working on collier boats between Newcastle, Whitby and London. Unhappy with his new career, by the beginning of 1861 he was back in Whitby as a fisherman. Not long after his return, Freeman was to make a name for himself by becoming the sole survivor of the lifeboat disaster of Saturday 9 February 1861, on his first lifeboat rescue, when the sea took twelve of the thirteen crew members. Henry was awarded his first decoration for bravery, the RNLI Silver Medal. On 24 October 1861, Freeman married Elizabeth Busfield (1835–98).

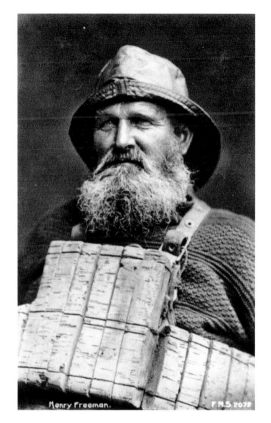

During his career as lifeboat-man, which spanned over forty years until his retirement in 1899, he rose through the ranks to become Coxswain of the No. 1 Lifeboat, first with service at the Upgang Lifeboat Station before transference to Whitby. During his tenure of service he saved some 300 lives and was decorated for gallantry numerous times by the RNLI and honoured throughout the land. Today the steps provide a wonderful short-cut to Cliff Street and the West Cliff from the harbour side and Haggersgate, and give a marvellous 'feel' of what the yards of the town would have been like, as it is almost unchanged from the days of James Lowell.

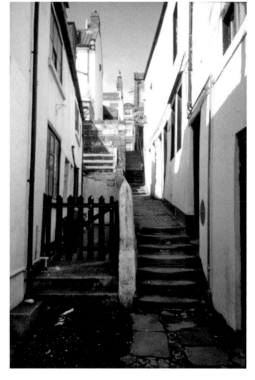

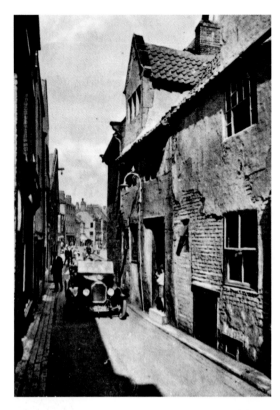

Haggersgate

Haggersgate is one of the most ancient roads of Whitby. Originally named by the Vikings, *Hakelsougate*, when they landed hereabouts, in 1296 it became *Haggleseygate*, meaning 'leading to the sea and cut in an irregular line'. It was described in 1817 by Reverend George Young in his *History of Whitby* as a most 'narrow and incommodious' highway, an opinion which was certainly valid until fairly recent times, particularly for the motorist before the one way traffic system was introduced, when some of the properties on the left of the postcard view were demolished, in the 1960s. Most of the houses in Haggersgate on the sea side, right, including the former Reading Room, were erected on wooden pilings driven into the sand as foundations, for this was the end of the town until developed in the sixteenth century. Haggersgate House, bottom, was built in 1760 by John Yeoman, a prominent ship owner, and it was described as the 'best brick house in town'. In 1817 Richard Rudyard lived here. He was a member of the family from which came the writer Rudyard Kipling. When first erected, the property faced onto the sands and was practically the last house in the town hereabouts. Today, it is used by the Mission to Seamen.

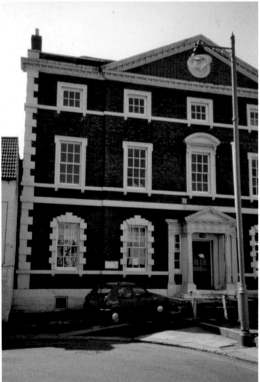

Black Horse Yard

What we know today as the Black Horse Inn with its Black Horse Yard, was originally the White Horse and White Horse Yard, not to be confused with what we now know as the White Horse Yard (then the White Horse and Griffin Yard). This situation often proved confusing and to end this confusion the White Horse inn changed its name at some date between 1823 and 1827 to the Black Horse, and with it the White Horse Yard became the Black Horse Yard. With this change the White Horse and Griffin assumed the simpler form of the White Horse, and its yard became the White Horse Yard. The MOH reported in 1909: 'The Black Horse Yard does not contain many houses, and these are satisfactory; but above the inhabited part of the yard there is an untidy condition, as is so often found in some of these yards, on account of the space being used for fowls, and also as a tipping ground for old pots, tins, pans, etc...In this yard, there is a manure heap that does not comply with the bye-laws, in that the cover over it is broken, and ought to be replaced by a new one.'

For many years the White Horse & Griffin was the Whitby terminus for the mail stagecoaches that left the town twice a week for York, commencing in 1783. Lord Normanby entertained Charles Dickens the writer for lunch here at Easter 1844. Dickens later wrote about the oyster shell grotto, which formed a feature in the yard.

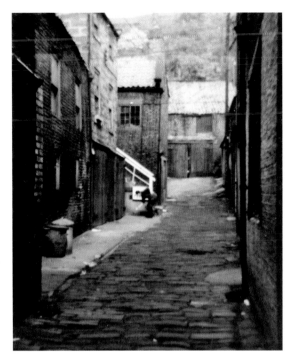

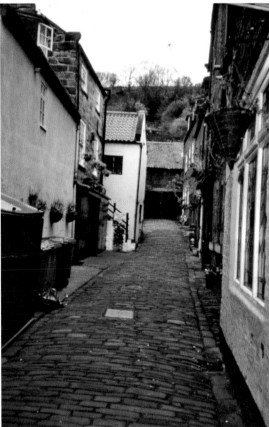

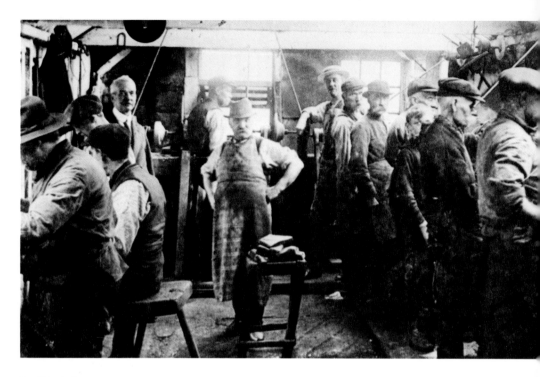

Jet Workshop

In 1874, while excavating foundations for a jet workshop in the Black Horse Yard, ancient objects from the old rubbish tip or 'midden' of Whitby Abbey were uncovered at the rear of the building. At one time, jet manufactory was one of the most important trades in the town. During one period, a quoits ground and drying ground also existed in the inn yard. In 1934, the club hut for the boy scouts could be found up Black Horse Yard. At that date, the owner of the yard was listed as Matthew Simpson.

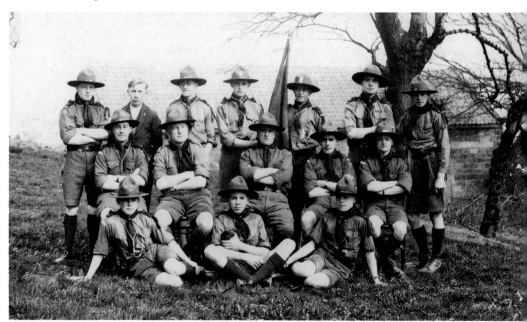

Barry's Yard off the Cragg

The Cragg was first an extension of Haggersgate and before 1690 was known as Burtry Cragg, after a type of alder tree [bourtree]. The main avenue was known as Scategate from the habit of hanging skate fish along it to dry. This was originally one of the rookeries of Whitby leading to many small yards tucked under the foot of the cliff and was densely populated (in 1817, 481 persons lived along here). Originally the houses had their backs (and privies) to the harbour, until 1786, when a landslip destroyed a large proportion of the properties immediately under the cliff. All the properties from the Magpie Café onwards were included in this radical re-orientation, and then a new staithe had to be created to give access to the 'new' fronts, represented today by Pier Road. On 10 January 1900 a further landslide demolished two houses and killed four persons; six others were injured. In 1909 the MOH reported 'It is very difficult to see how some of the houses on the Cragg can be very dry, as there are so many instances built near to, or adjacent to, the cliff side, from which water must drain through their walls; but, except in few instances, there is not much to find fault with. And there can be no doubt that the Cragg has vastly improved during the last few years, and this is especially so since the paving of cobbles was replaced by one of stone.'

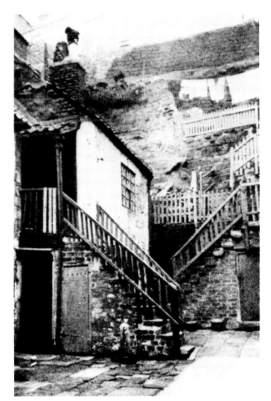

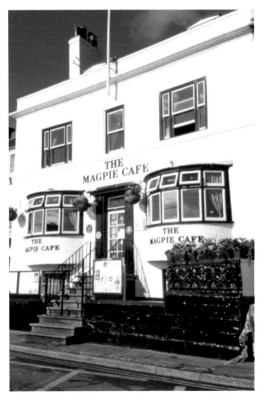

19

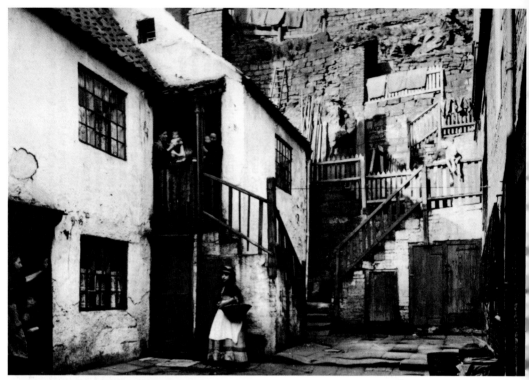

Barry's Yard off the Cragg

The MOH noted, 'A well-built block of buildings that are always kept clean and tidy. The house that was condemned at the top of the square is unoccupied; but there is only one privy to five houses, and the WC accommodation is being substituted.' The yard or square was pulled down in 1956 during wholesale demolition prior to the town redevelopment, which was so characteristic throughout England in that decade, with little foresight for the future. At one period a Lancasterian school room for girls was situated along the Cragg. Below are the remains of Barry's Yard as they are seen today.

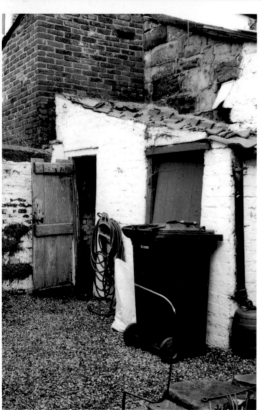

The Cragg Steps

Many of the houses on the Cragg that had suffered both earlier and on 10 January 1900, when a further landslide demolished two houses, killing Mrs A. Robinson (aged forty-three), Mrs Dina Turvey (aged twenty-five), Sarah Ann Turvey (aged fifteen months) and injured six others of which a Mrs Leaf died later on 22 January, remained derelict until slum clearance in the 1950s and 1960s. A great number of foundations and part-walls still remain visible even to this day, many forming small gardens. Today, the Cragg is accessible to the public and is a marvellous way to avoid the crowds along Pier Road. Entrance is gained at the bottom of Pier Lane and there are ginnels along Pier Road at various points giving access. By climbing the steps at the end, through an arch with wonderful views across the harbour to the East Side and the Abbey, it is possible to come out on Khyber Pass. An interesting ascent to the West Cliff with all its amusements can be had by way of these steps to the Khyber Pass, with a final view across to the East Side and the Abbey, through the stone arch which runs beneath Spion Kop. In 1909 the MOH wrote, 'Two unnamed yards that are very satisfactory, and the Cliff Steps, to which the same remark applies, bring us to the long yard with some very good and well-built houses at the end of the Cragg, where no fault can be found'.

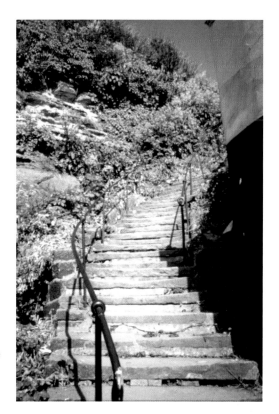

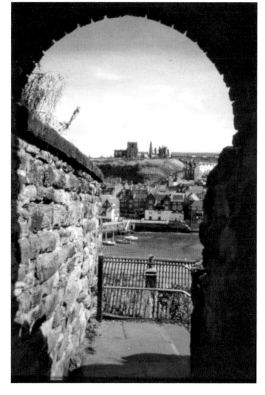

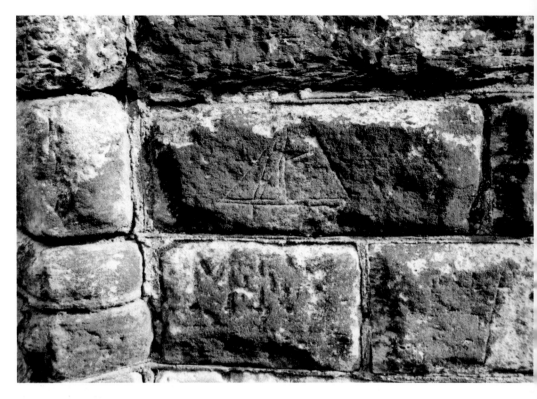

Khyber Pass

It is an artificial cutting made in about 1849 and used for getting building materials up to the West Cliff Estate, as there was previously no access onto the cliffs above. The headland to the right is known as 'Spion Kop', from the South African language 'spy hill' meaning 'look out'. The archway, mentioned previously, is just visible below the steps on the right, and on the left hand wall, as you enter, this charming piece of nineteenth-century graffiti of a ship, cut into the stonework, is found.

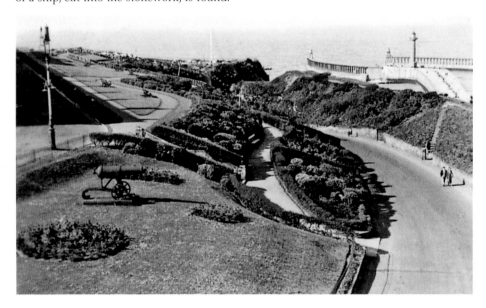

The Cragg & Streoneshalh House

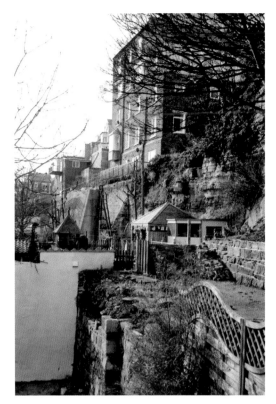

Both the names 'Khyber Pass' and 'Spion Cop' are taken from the period of the British Empire when the country had interests in India and the Commonwealth. The Khyber Pass is now the principal approach from the Pier to the West Cliff, which is dominated by the statue of Captain Cook and the Whalebone Arch. On Spion Kop, The Bram Stoker Memorial Seat is situated at the south end. This Victorian-style bench was placed here jointly by the Scarborough Borough Council and the Dracula Society in April 1980 to commemorate the link between the author and the town, and the inspiration derived from Whitby while writing chapters 6-8 of *Dracula*. The seat looks directly across the harbour to the East Cliff and from it every feature of the town mentioned in the novel is visible. An interesting sight along the Cragg is the view of the back of the house known as *Streoneshalh*, which from this angle appears as a huge six-storey building; but the front (bottom photograph) it is quite an amazing contrast! The word *Streoneshalh* is the old Nordic Scandinavian name for Whitby, and means 'white cliffs' – which is what they would no doubt have appeared to invaders as the entered the bay. In time, 'White Cliffs' became 'White Bay' which later gave us the name Whitby. At one period a photographer named Wallis had his studio in the right-hand side of this semi-detached frontage; and an artist had his studio in the lean to left hand-side.

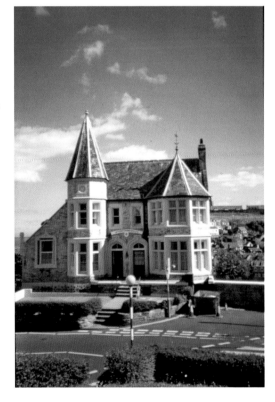

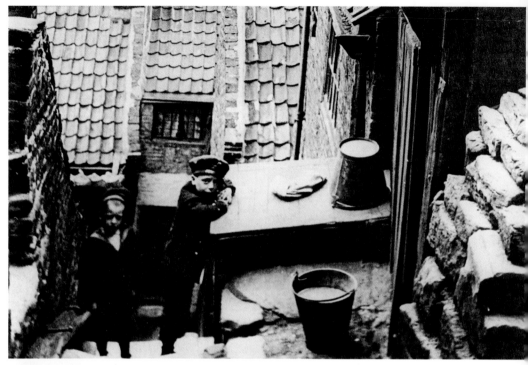

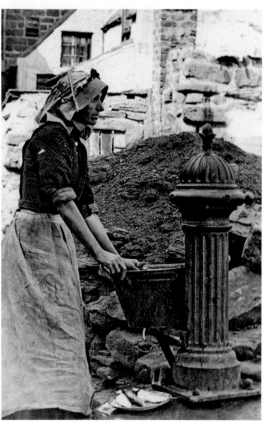

The Cragg

Above, two urchins watch as the photographer captures an unknown yard off the Cragg; notice the old galvanised tin buckets for fetching water. Below, a wonderful study of a Victorian lady washing fish at a pump on the Cragg known as 'Pier Pump', which once stood at the top of the small flight of steps called 'Pump Steps'. At this time it was the only public pump in the area. The nearest alternative public sources of water were the Bagdale Pump at the bottom of Union Road, and the Virgin Pump, situated at Alders Waste on the other side of the river.

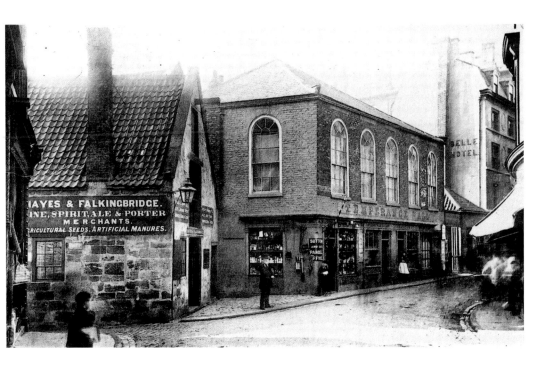

Baxtergate c. 1890

Photographed by Frank M. Sutcliffe, Falkinbridge's wine vault was the former chapel of ease known as the Chalice House that became redundant on the building of St Ninian's chapel further along the street, in 1778. This old chapel was finally pulled down for road widening in 1925. The Temperance Hall (with round-head windows) was demolished in 1905 to make way for the London Joint Stock Bank, which later became the Midland Bank before changing its name again. In between the cluster of buildings was a small yard which is seen over the roof tops (bottom).

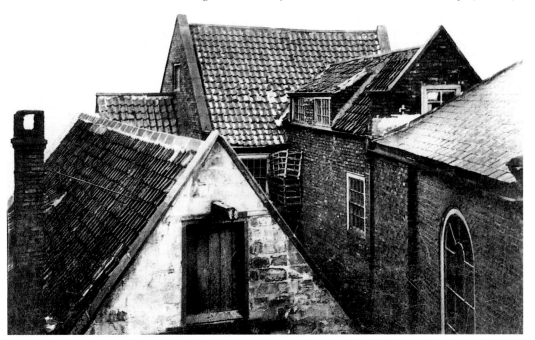

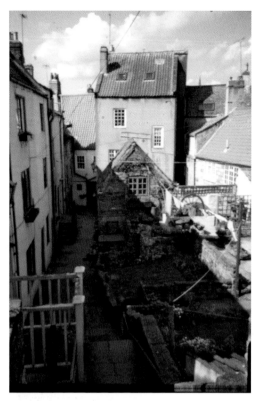

Blackburn Yard off Church Street

A view of Blackburn Yard, from the steps that lead up to the Donkey Road via Aelfleda Terrace. From above, is possible to see the missing property and how close the yards are, just one house width from its neighbour. It is known that two yards of this name existed off Church Street at the same date (1828), which must have been confusing. In 1909 the MOH wrote, 'Blackburn's Yard stands out with several others as having been wonderfully improved of late years. At one time, it was usual for the Inspectors and myself to find a very unsatisfactory state of affairs in this yard; the privies were bad, both structurally and also owing to the dirty habits of the persons who used them, and some of the houses required repairs. But today the privies have been repaired and are kept clean, the houses are in a very much better state, and, except for the steps, which want repairing, the yard is satisfactory. It will be remembered that the Council repaired the channel, and this has made a very good job of it.' This yard is one of the few with public access, and the 'Wash House Pottery' (bottom) takes its name from that facility in which it is housed. Continuing up the steps, past the site of Mary Linskill's birthplace marked by a plaque, there is a very interesting route to the abbey, with marvellous views back onto the roof-tops and across the harbour.

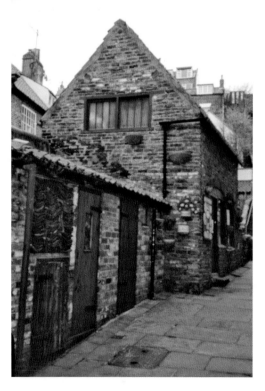

Borough Place, 96B Church Street

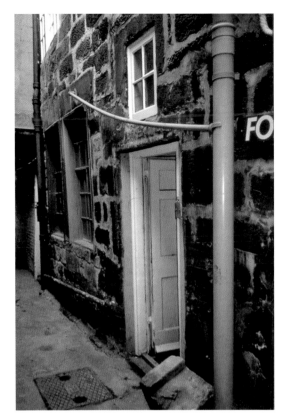

An interesting and somewhat convoluted yard, the first and oldest property near its entrance had carved over the door the date and initials 'W. A. L. 1618', for William and Elizabeth Linskill. In 1909 the MOH reported, 'there is little to find fault with, except the cobble stones used as paving at the bottom of the yard'. In 1934 the principal owners of Borough Place were said to be J. Falkenbridge, Parker & Hopperton. In recent times, the property has undergone conversion into flats with the tragic loss of many original ancient features. The insertion of the modern window destroyed the oval light and inscription (bottom drawing), which made room for a new door, but lost us the chamfered doorway details – vandalism! To add to this, oak-panelled Jacobean rooms inside had their woodwork torn out. Town dispensaries provided free medicines and medical treatment for the poor and were founded in many towns in the late eighteenth and nineteenth centuries. They were funded by donations and public subscription, subscribers having the right to nominate a number of poor patients for treatment. In Whitby the dispensary opened in 1786, in a building in Church Street that was demolished in the 1950s. However, for a period, from the study of deeds for 96B Church Street (Borough Place), it is clear the dispensary was at this address for a time.

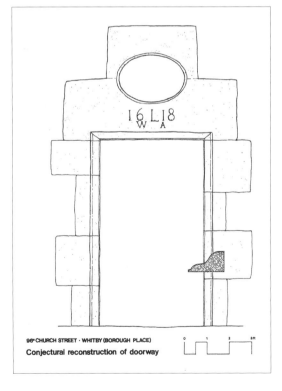

96ʰ CHURCH STREET · WHITBY (BOROUGH PLACE)
Conjectural reconstruction of doorway

27

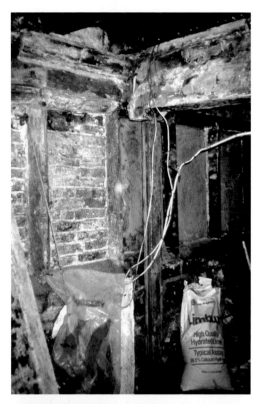

Borough Place, 96B Church Street

In the last decade, many of the older properties in Whitby have felt the hand of the builder as new owners buy them up as second homes or let as holiday cottages and modernise them to comply with planning and other regulations. As a consequence, there has been an increase in new architectural features coming to the surface as plaster and bricks have been swept away. This was the case with 96B Church Street, where up Borough Place, remedial work on the exterior revealed a series of fifteenth- or sixteenth-century mullion windows. The uncovering of these meant that historians had to rethink the history of this building in light of the new discovery, and it is clear that the date of this property is older than first estimated. At least the builders' and planners' advice was heeded and the ancient windows were left uncovered for the enjoyment of future generations. An interesting facet of early building history associated with Whitby which has come to light, is one of the many superstitious practices of past stonemasons and builders – walling a cat up in the chimney alive! Over the years the cat of course suffocates and, due to the heat, becomes mummified. Today, when a new fireplace is fitted, the desiccated bodies of these cats often tumble out of the stonework – giving fright to the young apprentice who may have been tasked with the fireplace removal.

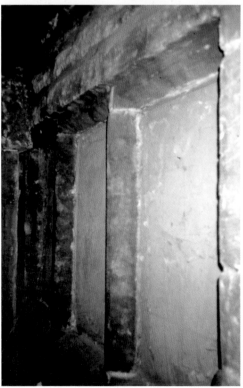

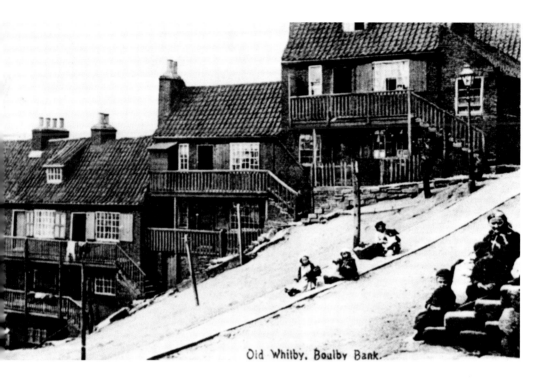

Old Whitby. Boulby Bank.

Boulby Bank, Church Street

This area took its name from Adam Boulby at an early date. The principal owner in 1837 was given as John Elgie. In 1909 the MOH wrote, 'Boulby Bank has on the left-hand side some of the objectionable cobblestones, which are frequently wet with soapsuds, etc. High Walk is now a clean and highly respectable part, and is an example of the way that tenants can keep their houses if the inclination to do so were there. The part of the bank opposite is just the reverse – I refer to the so-called Middle Walk...'

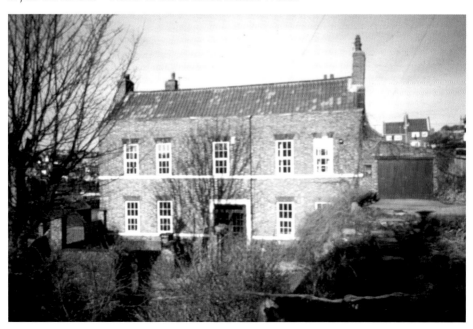

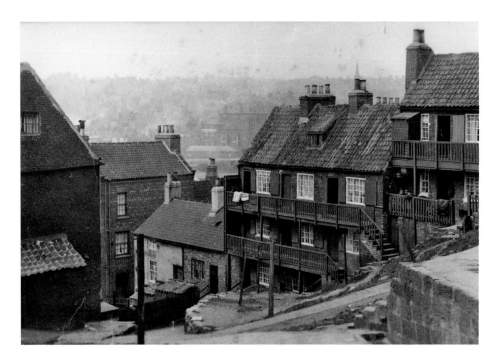

Boulby Bank & The Ropery

'... Middle Walk and although some of the houses have recently been white-washed, and don't look quite so bad as I have seen them, the repair of them leaves much to be desired; but, as the property has just changed hands, I don't think that it is wise to interfere until I see what line the new landlord is going to take. Low Walk is very badly paved with cobblestones, which badly require attention. The houses that I have condemned at the sea end of the walk are now in good repair.'

Below, is the original Ropery that gave its name to the street which ran along the top of Boulby Bank.

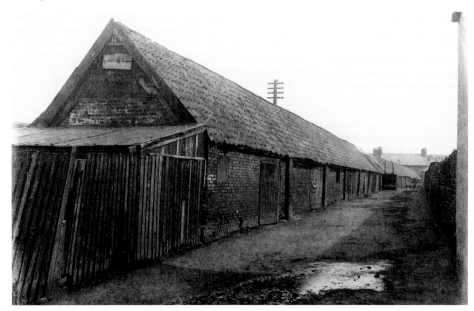

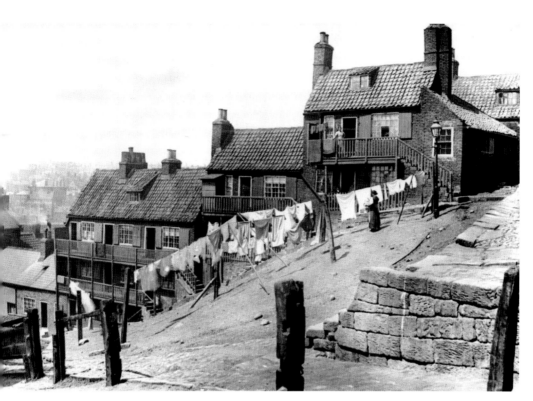

Old Boulby Bank

Among the properties up Boulby Bank in
the nineteenth century, was a cow house,
part of a ropery, and a bakehouse. There
was only one public tap for water, which
was reached by crossing the 'Drying
Green', which was said to be a difficult
task in wet weather when the ground was
slippy. By 1934, a separate listing existed
under the name of 'Boulby Bank Top',
principal owner Charles Usher. At the top
of Boulby Bank the large red-brick
mansion was formerly a manor house
of the town, and the brick façade of
eighteenth century date, possibly hides
an earlier timber-framed structure.

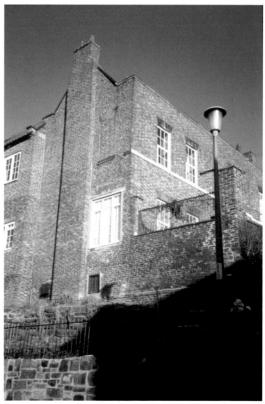

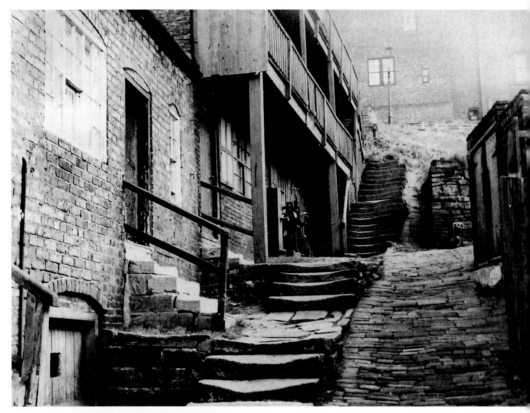

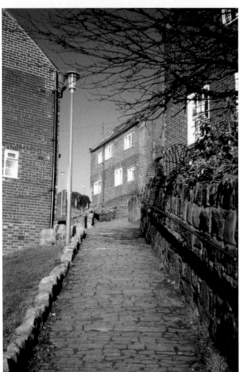

Bottom of Boulby Bank

Many of the buildings were finally demolished in 1955 and rebuilding took place almost immediately, providing high density council housing. Boulby Bank was much admired and visited by artists for its quaint and picturesque galleried houses that seemed to appear to defy gravity. Interestingly, because of the nature of the way properties were erected, the term 'flying freehold' developed for the housing here. This meant the owners of lower houses were not responsible for those immediately above and, in principal, you could knock down a property leaving the building on top in mid air – or 'flying'!

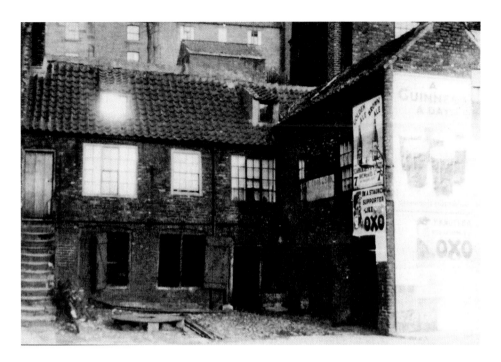

The Blacksmith

Mr Cook's blacksmith shop, is shown above, standing near the bottom of Boulby Bank in the 1930s, above which loomed the buildings of Lower Boulby Bank. There was plenty of work for blacksmiths and many specialised in producing and repairing metalwork for the ship-building industry. Of course, much of the principal work came from shoeing horses and repairing cart wheels etc., as this was still very much the era of the horse. The circular steel plate with the centre hole, seen below, was used for wheel making and shrinking the iron tyres on to the cart wheel.

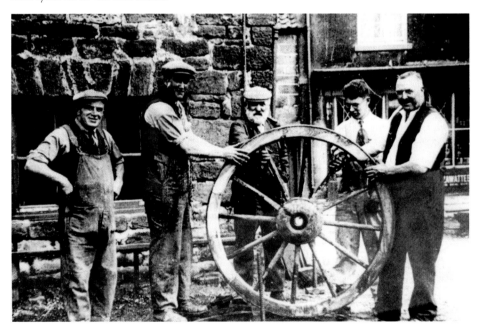

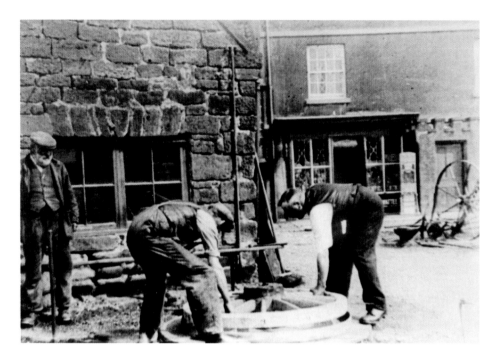

Hooping the Wheel

In early wheel-making, the blacksmith had a method of shrinking a complete band of iron onto the wheel. The finished wood sections were held together with a tool known as a 'Samson' that gripped the sections together in order to be able to nail on the final iron 'strake', one of a series of strips of iron nailed around the wheel to form a tyre. The names of the parts of a wheel are few and simple: the nave (hub), the spokes, the felloes (sections forming the perimeter) and the tyre.

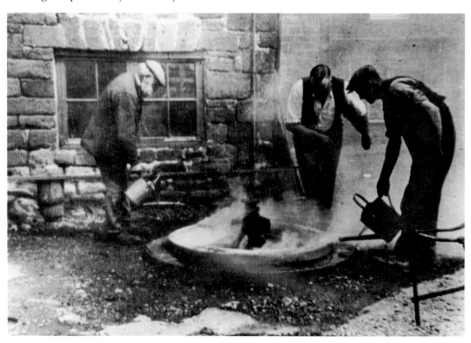

Breckon's Yard, Church Street

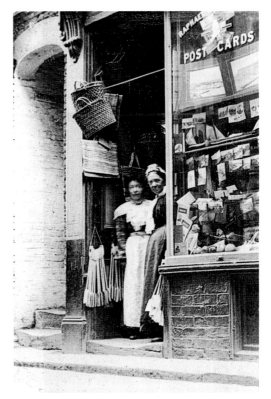

The Revd George Young in his work
A History of Whitby, Vol. II, published in
1817, described the town at an early date
and wrote: 'The ancient streets of Whitby
about the year 1600, and even in 1650, were
mere skeletons com-pared with what they
are now. In proportions to the increase in
population, and the consequent demand
for houses, the front ground was gradually
filled up with buildings, so as to form a
line of contiguous houses, on each side of
every street; leaving, at convenient intervals,
passages to the garths behind; and these
garths, having houses erected on them, were
converted by degrees into crowded yards.
In the oldest streets, viz. Church Street,
Grape Lane, Flowergate, Baxtergate, and
Haggersgate, great numbers of these yards
have been formed, distinguished by the
names of their principal owners, or by some
accidental circumstances. The extent of
these yards, and the intervals between them,
may give us some idea of the dimensions of
the tofts and half tofts of former ages.'

Over the centuries, many yards have
changed names. Others, of course, have
become lost through demolition and town
redevelopment, a process still occurring
even into the twenty-first century, but in
principle, what Young states above about
being able to discern the size of burgages
still holds true today. An example of name
changing can be seen here, when Breckons
Yard later became Foresters Court and was
dealt with under that name.

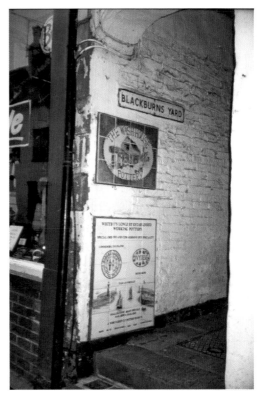

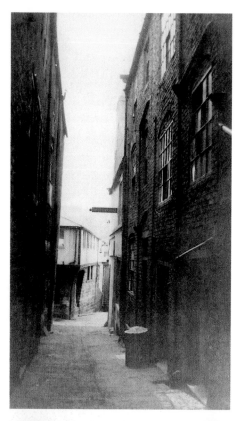

Brewster's Yard, Church Street

This yard, is more a street or ginnel rather than an enclosed yard. It was a continuation of Grape Lane, the end of which was known as the 'Shambles' as it was once an area full of butchers and slaughter houses. 'Shambles' is an old term often given to such districts, as can be observed in York for instance, which has the famous Shambles that was, in the medieval period, a street of butchers. The ginnel here at Whitby, photographed in 1939, ran from Grape Lane and connected to the Fish Pier on the east side. In the background is the old market hall, which can be seen in the lower photograph showing a passage running down the side that disappeared when public toilets were created in the market square. The market hall that survives today as an inn, above small retail units, and was erected during the Victorian period, closed after the Second World War, and it was then converted into a clothing factory for the famous Burberry Company. This was closed in the year 2001, and subsequently the market was sold into private ownership and turned into a craft centre and restaurant in the following year, with the introduction of the *Heartbeat Museum* into the property. For some years after Burberry maintained a clothing outlet shop in the market place, which opened in the same year as the factory closed. Whitby was granted a Charter for holding a market as early as 1445. Previous to that year the market had been held on a Sunday, but from what date is unknown. The Charter, however, changed the day to Saturday.

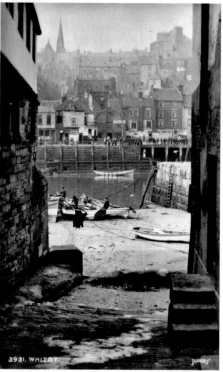

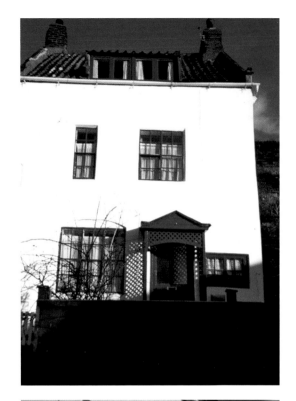

Clark's Yard off Church Street

In 1909, the MOH wrote 'Clark's Yard is in very good condition, and the privies are in good repair, and the yard is altogether very much improved'. This is true even today and the residents obviously take some pride in its cleanliness. At the very top of Clark's Yard stands this eighteenth-century cottage. The yard, however, extended beyond this property and a set of stone steps alongside it disappear into thin air as the houses above either fell or were taken down. An interesting feature are the 'Yorkshire Sash' windows. These differ from normal sash windows that slide up to open and are held in that position by a balanced weight by being placed sideways. As a consequence there is no need for the lead weights and rope which balances the normal sash window and prevents it from sliding down. The introduction of the Yorkshire Sash came about from the legendary thriftiness of the Yorkshireman who likes to save a 'bob or two' by any means he can!

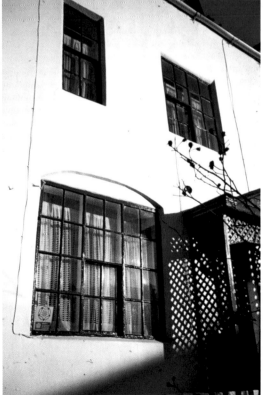

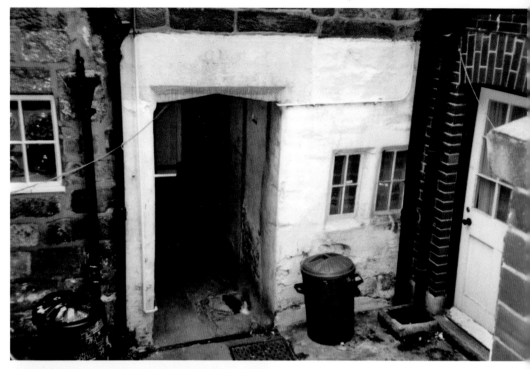

12A Cliff Street

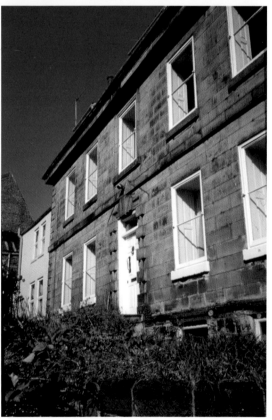

Behind a distinctive studded street door marked 12A (page 71) the visitor steps back in time when they pass through this seventeenth century doorway are confronted with *Paddock House* whose doorway is dated a century later to 1745. Untouched by the hand of builders, changing fashions have passed it by and in isolation it stands as the day it was built retaining is heavy Gibb's surrounds to windows and doors a magnificent example of Jacobean period architecture. Possibly owned by a merchant and slave trader, there is a cellar complete with manacles to which 'blacks' were shackled before being sold on.

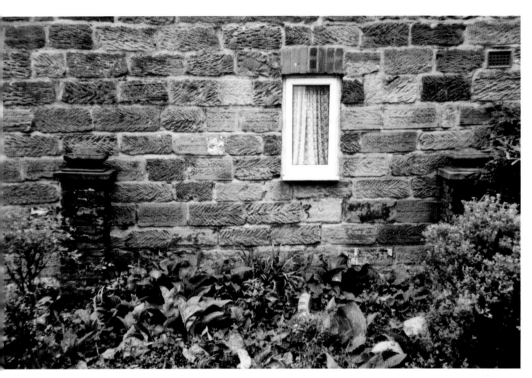

Now You See It – Now You Don't!

An interesting aspect of Paddock House is the stone gate pillars standing directly opposite the imposing house door, which are today placed against the gable end of housing in McLacklin's Yard which is on a lower level! This suggests that when Paddock House was first built, the ground in front was open and a flight of steps lead up from the yard to the property – the view then from Paddock House would have been a lot different as it overlooked Flowergate. Residents would be able to watch the comings and goings of the neighbourhood and those passing by could look up to the big house!

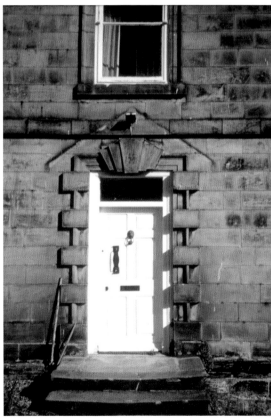

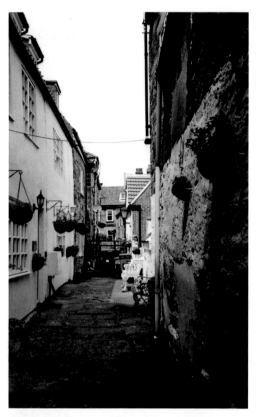

McLacklin's Yard

Looking along McLacklin's Yard it is possible to see 12A Cliff Street across the end; there is no doubt that in 1745 this yard did not exist and the land was filled in with housing after this date. The property with the satellite dish also dates from *c.* 1745 and was probably accommodation for the servants of 12A Cliff Street when this area was the entrance for the 'grand house'. It is also probable that there would have been stabling for a horse and coach completing an open-ended courtyard facing onto Flowergate. In 1909, the MOH reported McLacklin's Yard as being 'always a difficult yard to deal with. Only a short time ago, the Inspector and myself got the yard paved in the greater part of its length, and we have frequently had to take steps to have some defect put right. The privy accommodation is insufficient, and steps have had to be taken to have something done to remedy this defect. Notices have been served on some owners of the property, and they have been told to put in a sufficient number of privies or substitute WCs for these. There are one or two old disused houses in the yard which are very dirty and serve to act as tips for the neighbours; and there is a wash-house that is in a very filthy condition.'

In 1899, among the residents was an iron worker, a carter, a labourer, two [black]smiths, a jet worker, a boatman, a cab driver, and a mason.

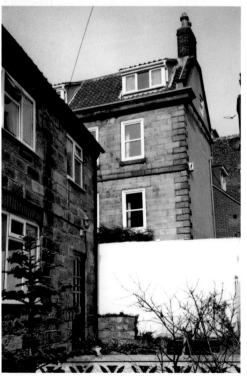

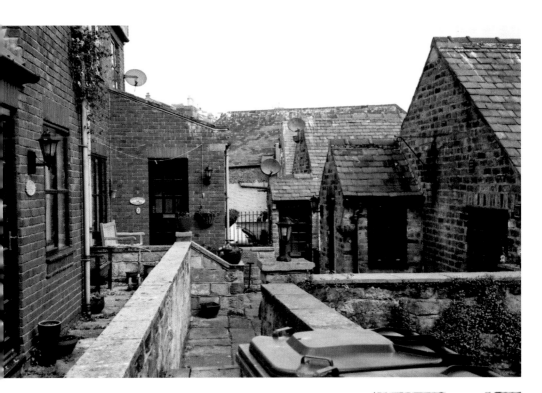

Easterby's Yard, Flowergate leading to Spenceley Yard off St Anne's Staithe

In 1909, the MOH noted, 'in Easterby's Yard, there is a very nice block of property, which is very much out of repair and badly wants some alterations, structurally, doing to it. In addition to this, the privies are very poor and want constant supervision to keep them in anything like decent order. They certainly have a very low sanitary standard.'

In 1931 the principal owner was Esther Robinson. Today Easterby's Yard (above) has had much property removed and rebuilt and turning right at the end you can gain access to Spenceley Yard via the wrought iron steps (below).

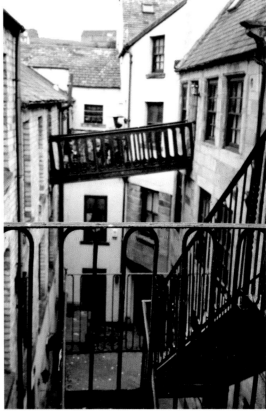

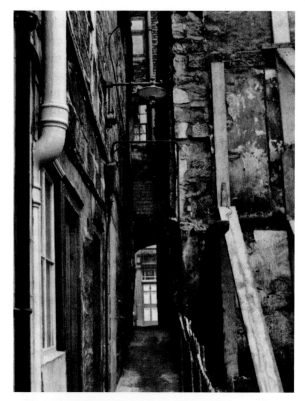

Ellerby Lane, Church Street

This lane connects Sandgate and Church Street which can be seen at the top of the upper photograph. It was once known as Anningson's Lane from a family of that name, and continued at its lower end across Sandgate and went down to the harbour via a flight of stone steps. It was connected to St Ann's Lane, next to the former Woolworth's building across the waters by a series of stepping stones. The walled up entrance on Sandgate, nos. 3–4, is still clearly visible and just seen on the extreme left of the bottom image. It is in this small space the fish market stood. Despite its apparent narrowness, this byway had a considerable number of properties down its length and in 1934 the warehouse and stables for the Co-operative stores, then situated on Sandgate, seen in the bottom photograph, stood up Ellerby Lane. The members of the Co-op at that date include Phil Hogarth (extreme left), Ted Parker (wearing apron) and Willy Tor (young man wearing apron). The Co-operative Store was first established in Whitby on Sandgate between 1887 and 90 where it traded as the Whitby Working Men's Co-operative Industrial Society. Later it transferred to premises in Wellington Road, built in the late 1930s with other departments in Baxtergate, some of which shut down in the early 1990s. The present Co-op 'superstore' was built on Langbourne Road in 1996 and forms part of the much larger North East & Cumbrian Co-op Industrial Society.

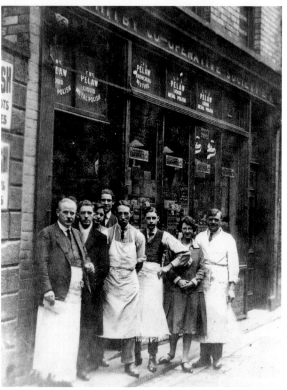

Forester's Court, Church Street

Once known as Breckons Yard, this yard took its present name from the Royal Antediluvian Order of Buffaloes (the 'Buffs' RAOB) who have a meeting hall at the top end, and who were named as the principal owners in 1934. The MOH recorded in 1909, 'Forester's Court is a large yard, with plenty of air space, and is in excellent condition'. For a period I had rooms in the Georgian property fronting onto Church Street – its entrance was through the arched entrance on that street and it had an ancient coloured glass sign above in green, red and gold displaying the name of the yard. In 1899, in Foresters Court lived William Matson, a tailor; Charles Gibson, a jet worker; and a Mr A. Wheatley, who was described as 'bridgeman', which no doubt meant that he was one of the operators of the old town swing bridge which is nearby. From records, the early structures were drawbridges and 'Bridgemasters' were appointed to collect the dues for vessels going above the bridge, and the rents of several tenements erected on the frameworks of the bridge. For Young, 'our bridge like the ancient London Bridge, was then encumbered with tenements built on it, some of which extended across its whole breadth, leaving an arched passage below'. The bridge Wheatley worked on, however, was the swivel bridge built in 1835, to a design by Francis Pickernell, at a cost of £10,000. This was replaced in 1909 with the present electrically operated swing bridge.

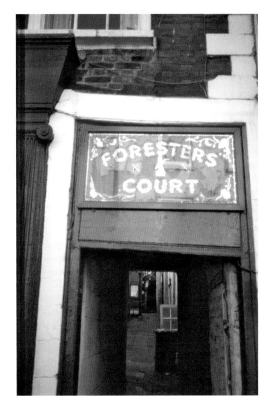

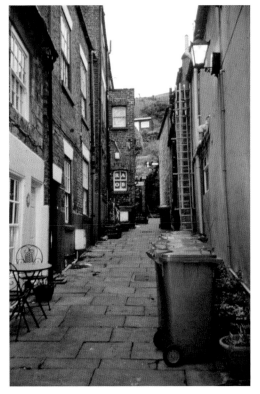

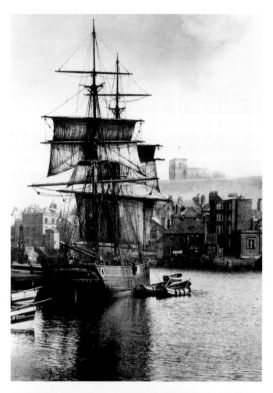

Greengates, Grape Lane

From across the harbour it is easy to spot the tallest building in Whitby standing on Grape Lane and rising up above its neighbours. Sandgate was first recorded by that name in 1426, and was a continuation of Grape Lane on the other side of Bridge Street, known as the 'Low Streets'.

A number of the buildings on Grape Lane were formerly banking houses; this gave it the local name 'Lombard Street' in the satirical literature of the period. In the tall property known as 'Greengates', from the colour of the gate (see next page), the tallest window in England can be found, containing no less than sixty panes of glass, which because of its distinct shape is known as a 'bottle window'. A number of others can be found in the town – two of note on Upgang Lane. Bottle windows are a feature of Whitby and were a device to avoid paying window tax. In many parts of England, windows were blocked to avoid paying this tax, but here in Whitby the legendary meanness of the Yorkshireman came up with the idea of extending the staircase window up the entire length of the building, this only counted as one window, but still allowed daylight to light the stairs. Along with Yorkshire Sash windows it showed how the thrifty Yorkshireman could save a 'bob or two!' Now in private ownership it still contains the original safe the size of a room, with its massive door.

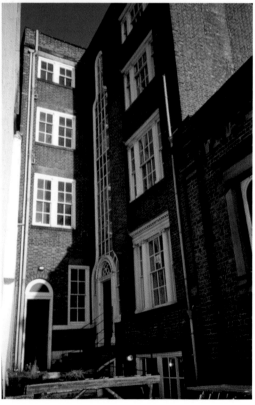

Greengates, The Bank

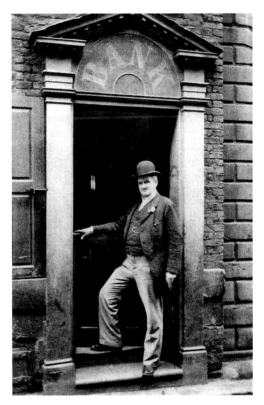

Grape Lane was at one period an important street containing most of the banking houses of the town. Greengates was the bank of Simpson, Chapman & Co., and the bank itself gained the name 'Green Gate' from the gate that closed off the premises at night, seen opposite. The bank was established in 1785 and closed its doors in 1901 when it amalgamated with the London & Joint Stock Bank and moved across onto the West Side. The 'green gate' was reputed to have been preserved until recent years in the vault of one of the present local banks. Prior to 1775, there are no records of any banking houses in the town. This is not necessarily surprising, as throughout the entire country only twelve banks are recorded in 1750 outside of London and a few major cities. The bank of Simpson, Chapman & Co. was founded by Wakefield Simpson, a draper, grocer and banker, in premises in the market place, Church Street. In about 1785, he took a partner, Abel Chapman, a wealthy inhabitant of Whitby. Together they opened the regular banking in Grape Lane. The two families were members of the Society of Friends' – Quakers – and by marriage many of the two families were married into other English banking families such as the Gurney's, Barclays and Fry's.

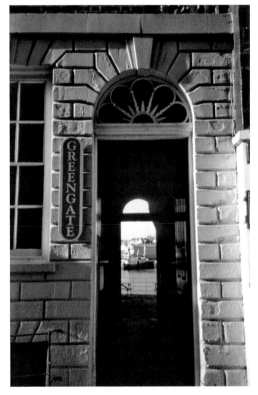

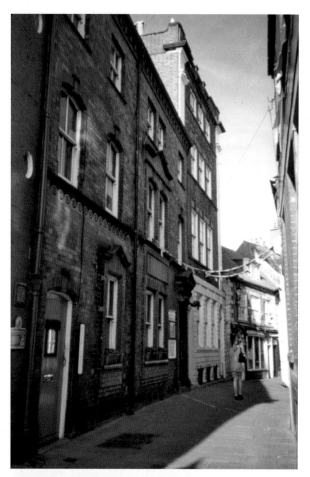

The Old Clinic, Grape Lane

Next door to Greengates is the red brick building of the clinic, which at one period also incorporated the house that is now the Captain Cook Museum. At the time of the clinic, the NHS did not exist and it was a private institution. The phasing out of these little cottage hospitals was one of the more regrettable consequences of the NHS policy of concentrating medical care in large complexes. Whitby Hospital at this time had just three surgical beds. The bottom photograph shows the woman's ward in 1905; it was sent by a patient to Miss Bowron of Church Street, Whitby.

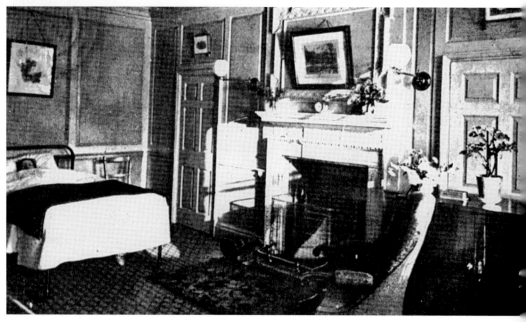

Sandgate & Lockey's Yard

(Left) Adjacent to Greengates in Grape Lane is Lockey's Yard and over the doorway of the principal cottage are the initials and date 'W. E. L. 1669' for William and Elizabeth Lockey. In 1909, the MOH wrote, 'Lockey's Yard is well-paved, and on the whole, is fairly satisfactory'. Grape Lane and Sandgate were often referred to as the 'Low Streets'. Grape Lane is a continuation of Sandgate beyond Bridge Street that cut through the two at a later date. Sandgate was first mentioned in the year 1401, and was a considerable street by 1592, so-named because it led to and bordered on the 'east sands'. Sandgate in 1817 was said to measure 73 yards to the market place, and, if extended to Brewster Lane, about 110 yards. The cross streets leading direct from Church Street towards the harbour, of which Ellerby Lane forms one, are also very short and, at the date mentioned, none of them exceeded 55 yards in length. The 'Low Streets' are narrow, even today, and are in some places scarcely 4 yards broad. Apart from Ellerby Lane, there were also a number of Yards off Sandgate, some of which remain intact, principally Nicholson's Yard between Nos. 5 and 6. Two of the other yards in Sandgate were Gray's Yard and Johnson's Yard. In the yard between Nos. 11 and 12 Sandgate, there is a cottage bearing the date 1743. Sandgate was for many years a street of butchers and its northern end was often referred to as the 'Shambles'.

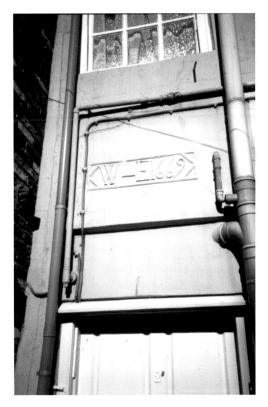

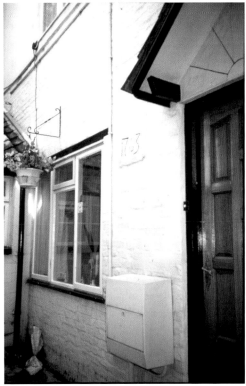

47

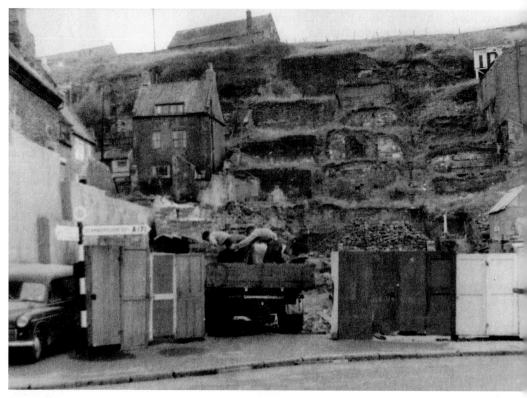

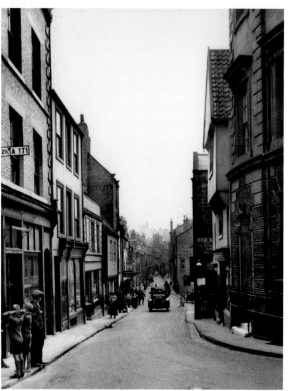

Green's Yard, Church Street
Above, the demolition of Green's Yard of Church Street as it bends around from Bridge Street in May 1955. The foundations of numerous former dwellings can be seen in the terraces behind. In 1934, the only named property belonged to Wilcocks Stores Ltd. And at No. 3 lived Robert Weatherill and his neighbour at No.4 was Henry Goodwill. The second building to the right is part of a sixteenth-century timber-framed merchant's house said to be the oldest secular building in the town; this was part demolished to build the former Quaker meeting house next building along.

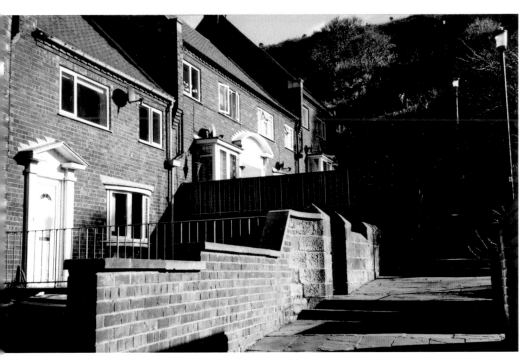

Green's Yard & Caedmon Steps

In 1995, Whitby gained an addition to the extensive heritage of ghauts and lanes. From Greens Yard as it is today, above, near the junction of Bridge Street and Church Street, a flight of sixty-five stone steps was built by the British Trust for Conservation Volunteers. Named 'Caedmon's Trod', after Whitby's famous cowman poet who lived at the abbey in the seventh century, these are an alternative route to the abbey other than the 199 Steps. Well worth the climb, this new ascent offers a fresh vantage point from which to appraise the town's endlessly fascinating townscape with its yards, lanes, steps and all.

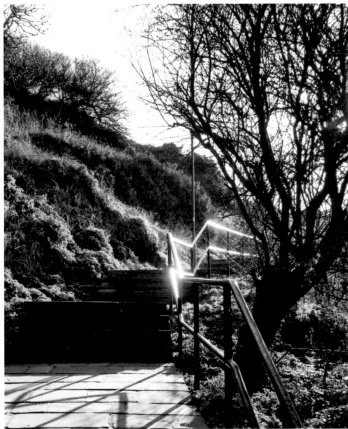

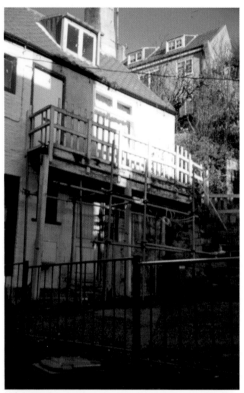

Ivy Yard, Church Street

In 1909, the MOH recorded 'Ivy Yard is one of the yards that is more or less damp; it lies near to the hillside, and there is not sufficient ventilation and air for it to be anything but damp except in very dry weather'. In 1934, the owner was Isaiah Bourdas. Today the yard is one of the few to still retain its wooden galleries to the upper cottages, although these appear to be being replaced. In the yard in 1899, lived William Evans, driller; Thomas Skidd, iron worker; James Russell, riveter; Mrs Kipling; and James Little, ironmonger.

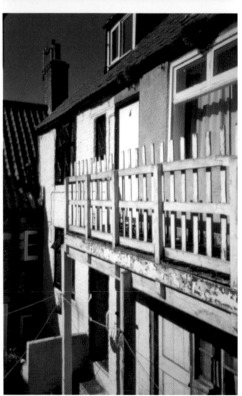

Johnson's Yard & Leng's Yard

Two yards separated by only the width of a brick wall; Johnson's Yards is to the left and Leng's Yard to the right. There appears to be no description of these yards by the MOH in 1909. Today, the yard appears to have altered little, but has been beautified with the addition of colourful hanging baskets. In 1899, the residents of four of the properties in Johnson's Yard included Alfred Frank, jet worker; Mrs Mary McGrafth; Mrs Hannah Cryrer, laundress; and William Elders, confectioner. In 1934, Henry Pinder owned the yard and there were five named occupants including Mary Frank, who may have been the widow of Alfred or a daughter. In 1899, Leng's Yard had a joiner, a labourer, a stonemason and an outside porter living there. In 1934 Leng's yard was occupied by John R. Young, Mary Hudson and George Hudson who lived at No. 3 and No. 4 respectively, and the property was owned by W. G. Hudson – family relationships were often convoluted in Whitby, and no doubt the Hudson family was a genealogical nightmare! Lastly, at No. 5 lived William Cowey in property owned by Sir John Harrowing of Stakesby House, senior member of an important ship-building and banking family.

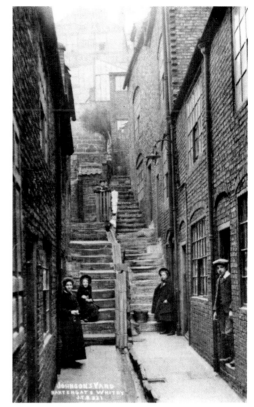

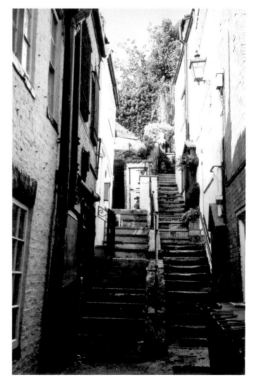

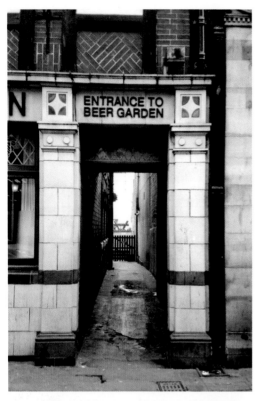

The Yard Gates

At the time of the yards in the late Middle Ages and later periods, there was of course no organised police force and as such residents along the yards often locked themselves in at night – many of the yards had a stout gate for this purpose.

None of the original yard gates exist. Today, however, it is noticeable that with an influx of wealthy second-home owners who cherish their privacy, they are paying for new modern wrought-iron gates like that now fronting Johnson's Yard in the form of two spouting whales. Across the way, the yard adjacent to the wet fish shop also has a new wrought-iron gate of modern design. Of course some yards cannot be gated, like the yard adjacent to the Plough Inn on Baxtergate, whose original frontage is protected by planning regulations. The premises of the present day inn is an enlargement of the original public house which was known in 1797 as 'Speed the Plough', perhaps a corruption of that saying 'God Speed the Plough'. It reminds us that Whitby was, before being a major seaport, a market town of some repute at that date. In 1837 the owner was John Bovill (landlord Richard Hilton) and the rateable value was 11s 5d; it was then listed as the Plough Inn from this period. The original main entrance was down the narrow passage from Baxtergate, known as Plough Inn Yard. In 1904 the police endeavoured to close the Plough on the grounds of poor accommodation.

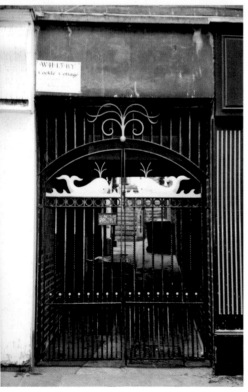

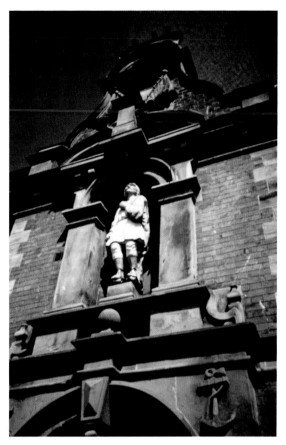

The Seaman's Hospital, Church Street
Founded in 1675, the Seaman's Hospital was designed to assist distressed seamen, and to provide relief for their widows and the education of their children. The present building was established on its site in the eighteenth century, but the façade dates only from 1842 and was built to a design by Sir George Gilbert Scott. In 1995, there was extensive exterior restoration and remodelling of interior. This also led to the replacement in fibreglass of the figure in the central niche, a copy of the original figurehead from the boat the *Black Prince*. Behind this noble exterior lay three yards.

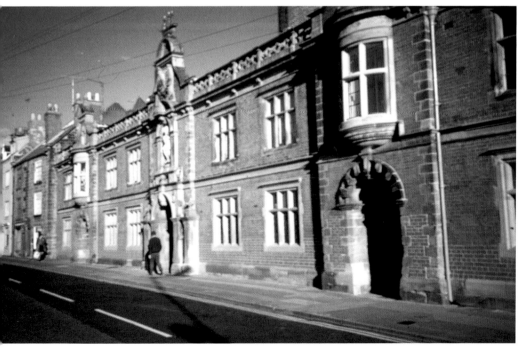

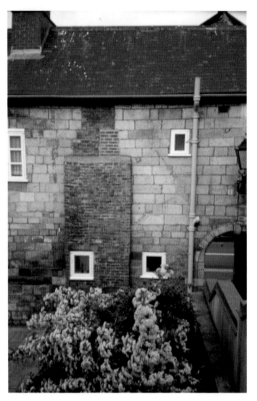

The Seaman's Hospital

'First Hospital Yard has bad cobble stone, and, when I was there in the earlier part of the year, the channel was very bad. I reported this to the Surveyor and he had it repaired. Some very considerable and necessary repairs have been done at the top of the yard since the property changed hands.'

'Low Hospital Yard at the lower end is in very good repair, but at the top end there is a stack of property that I condemned in 1906 and nothing has been done to it till now. I wrote to the owner some short time ago, as it was becoming a sort of tip for the whole neighbourhood. Since that time it has been decided to rebuild the houses and, in order to make a start, forty loads of rubbish had to be removed. I think that, when the alterations are made, the houses will be nice dwellings.'

'Middle Hospital Yard is at present having the consideration of the Trustees for the Seamen's Hospital dwellings, who hope to do some repairs shortly. The houses, speaking generally, are not in a very bad condition, but they are small according to our present-day way of looking at things, but as they are, in most cases, inhabited by only one person, there is probably sufficient room for them...During the year, I have had some letters about these houses which contained very exaggerated statements and, although I do not say that they are up to modern requirements, I have no doubt that many of the inhabitants could live happily and healthily in them for many years to come.'

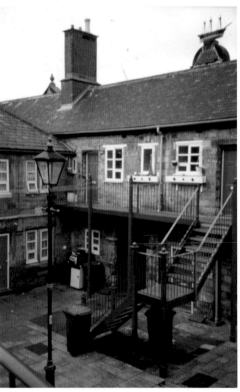

Kiln Yard

Kiln Yard photographed by Tom Watson
showing 'Possers' in the galvanised
wash tubs. The history of this yard
includes an early reference dated 1655
concerning 'Thomas Barker, of Stair
foote, at Whitby, be suppressed for
keeping a common ale house [here] for
three years'. In 1723, a lease naming Jane
Wilson specifies that there be 'sufficient
water for steeping barley to make
malt in this kiln and in the low kiln in
Whitby for family use in her dwelling
house'. In 1909, the MOH reported, 'Kiln
Yard is in a very bad state; the channel
and the paving are bad. In this yard
there is a stack of property, consisting of
three tenements and two jet-shops that
are in a shocking state of repair, one of
them in particular, being disgraceful. On
my advice, the owners were served with
a notice requiring them to put it into
a habitable repair. The roof has been
taken off, new beams put in, and there
is every indication that the property
will be made satisfactory early in the
New Year'. In both 1828 and 1934, there
was a separate yard known as Kiln
Entry, which along with Kiln Yard was
probably named for its association with
the malt kiln which stood hereabouts.
In 1934 the property was owned by the
Whitby Housing Association. Bottom,
Hall's Yard, off Flowergate, which was
formerly called Duck's Yard from a
family of that name – a lovely almost
untouched eighteenth-century property.

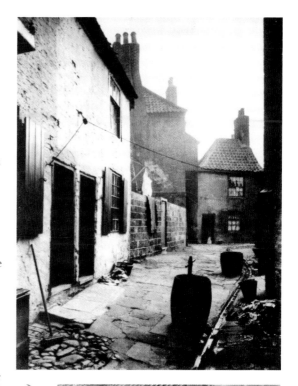

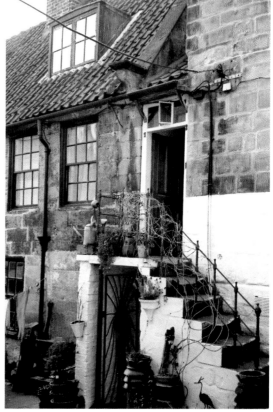

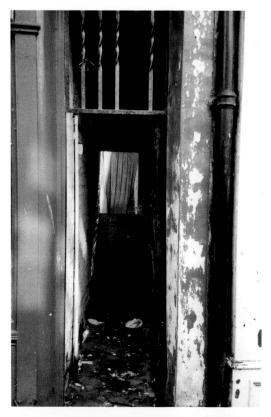

Lee's Yard, Baxtergate

In 1909, the MOH reported, 'In Lee's Yard, in which the houses were situated which I condemned some time ago, there is now a very nice warehouse and the yard looks clean and tidy'. Today, Lee's Yard is more an entrance porch for seemingly a single dwelling or perhaps a small number of flats above the shops. In reality, it can hardly be classed as a yard now. Up until late 2011, it still retained its original marble name plate on the wall, but I noticed today that this is now missing. In 1899, only two occupants are named, E. Barnett, labourer and William Ruehorn, iron worker. Situated as it is on Baxtergate, this street was mentioned as early as 1401 and is so named from a family called Baxter who owned property here from early times. Baxtergate was almost purely a residential street until about the year 1700, and is built upon a sandbank that followed the contours of the river; indeed, old mooring-posts have been discovered during excavations. The route today is slightly less curved than the original line due to extensive redevelopment in modern times. The present day Baxtergate is the principal shopping street, and entirely pedestrianised, but it was at one time open to two-way traffic. From 9 June 1887, Baxtergate began to be widened at the east end, at which time the Talbot Hotel and adjoining property was put back to create more space. In 1925, the road was again widened near the Midland Bank end.

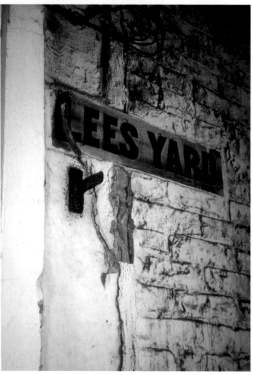

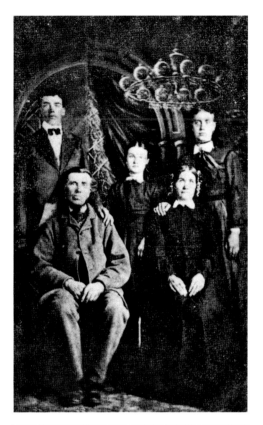

Linskill Square

This yard took its title from Reuben Linskill, who was an ancestor of the famous Whitby authoress Mary Linskill. Reuben Linskill (who died before 1726), a Quaker, was noted for his public spirit, hospitality, plainness and simplicity of manners. It is said that the Duchess of Buckingham when in the North, always visited Reuben's and nowhere else in this part. Mary Linskill (1840-91) was one of the town's native author's of romantic novels set in Whitby. The top photograph shows Mary as a child sat between her mother and father. The cottages up Blackburn's Yard, in one of which Mary was born, were damaged by a storm in 1950 and were subsequently demolished. Mary's father, Thomas Linskill, was the town Constable for many years and at one period, an early police station was situated in Linskill Square before a purpose-built one was erected in Victoria Square in 1854. The police station may have been situated in the premises recorded as a schoolroom and tenement in 1837. The MOH reported in 1909, 'Linskill Square is a large, well-paved yard and is probably one of the best in the town'. In 1934, the United Auto-mobile Company owned No. 6A and for many years the Bus Drivers' Rest Room was found here.

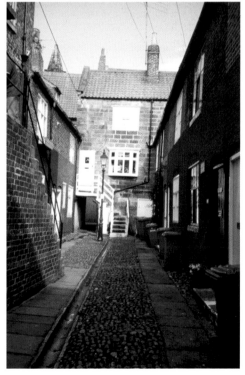

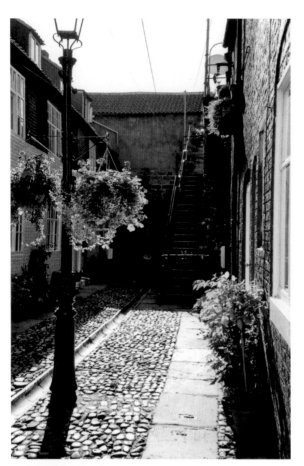

Linskill Square

Said to be the best yard in town in 1909, the same can be said today. Linskill Square is worth a visit being open to public and a short-cut from the present bus station (in Victoria Square) onto the main shopping street Baxtergate. Entrance is via an ornate wrought-iron gate. During the medieval period, most yards and squares had a gate which was locked at night as security to keep out the rougher element of the town, and a number of new gates are being installed at the entrance to the yards. Below, is the grave of Mary Linskill in St Mary's churchyard.

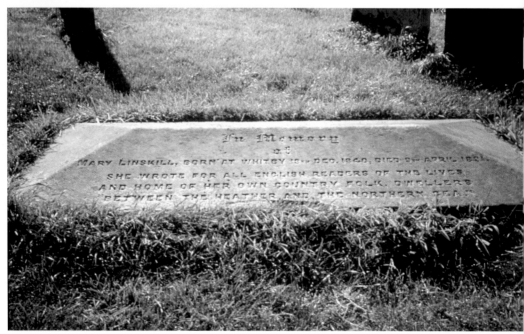

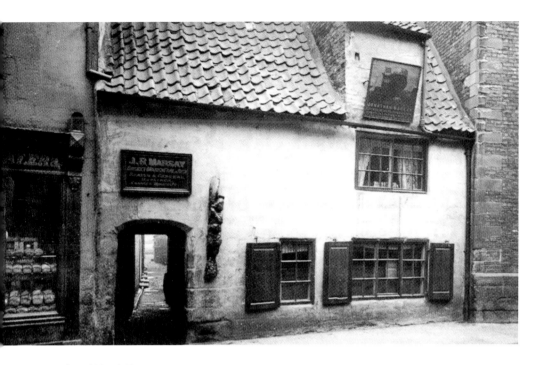

Loggerhead Yard, Baxtergate

Formerly known as Doctor Lane, this is the Baxtergate entrance. What is today the Smuggler's Café, was originally The Old Ship Launch Inn *c.* 1740–1915, and reputedly the haunt of smugglers, dating back to the early fifteenth century. On the Baxtergate façade is a wooden carved figure that is a ship's figurehead – known as a loggerhead – and it was this piece of nautical furniture which gave its name to the yard that has lettered above the low entrance arch 'Duck or Grouse'! It was once connected with another inn at the other end of Loggerhead Yard by a smugglers' tunnel.

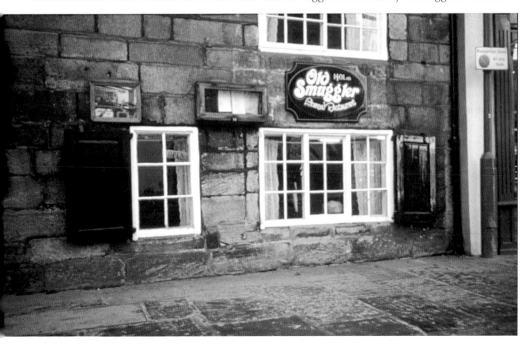

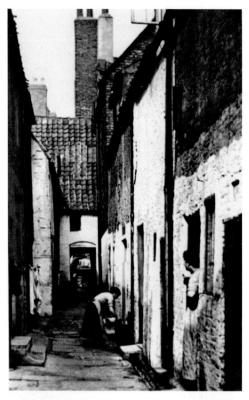

Loggerhead Yard

This postcard shows the view along
Loggerhead Yard toward Baxtergate and the
arched entrance. Interestingly, recent work
has revealed that Loggerhead Yard at some
date was also named Church Walk and the
inscribed street name has been left uncovered
in the newly plastered wall. In 1909, the
MOH wrote of the yard, 'Now much better
than it used to be, and the houses are in
fairly good repair and the privies are clean
and structurally good, although they are very
close to the houses. The channel in the yard
is also in need of repairs. The urinal at the
top is often a nuisance in warm weather'.
Loggerhead Yard was always a populous yard
with about twenty properties. In 1837, the
yard's address was given as Dock End, and it
was noted that Richard Hilton had a stable
and warehouses here. William Turnbull had a
dwelling house, stable and blacksmith's forge
here and Robert Jackson occupied a tenement
with kitchen and workshop. Mary Robinson
and William Shaw lived in properties owned
by the estate of Mr T. Galilee. In 1899, there
was still a blacksmith in the yard, and the
occupations of other residents included
a carter, cab driver, NE Railway porter,
warehouseman, coal dealer, tailor, carpenter,
jet worker and three labourers. In 1934, most
of the property in Loggerhead Yard appears to
be owned by John Taylor and the majority of
property was rated at four or five shillings.

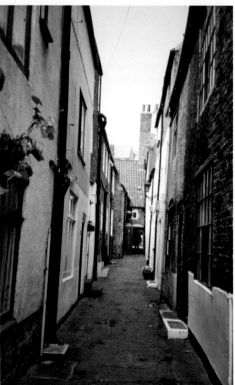

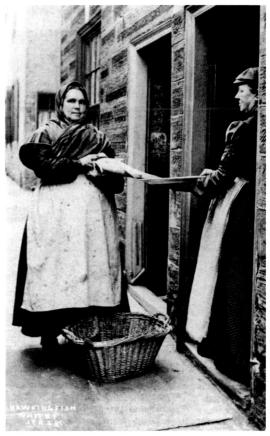

The Fish Seller

A J. T. Ross postcard showing Dolly, the wife of Whitby fisherman Tom Gaines. She had a fish stall, but towards the day's end, she was happy to hawk any remaining fish around the streets and yards. In the home, fish would be baked, fried, boiled, simmered in milk, or grilled beside the open fire using a gridiron – and fish pie was considered a special delicacy. Below, the inscribed yard nameplate, uncovered during work on the yard, was left exposed and clearly states 'Church Walk', showing that this yard as been known by at least three different titles.

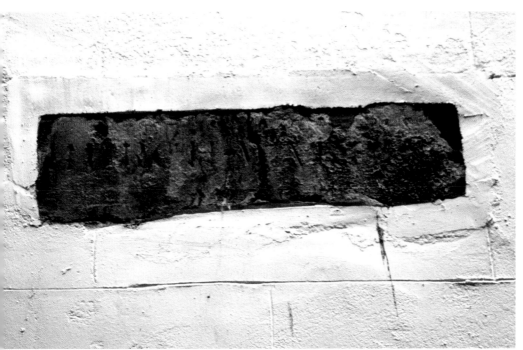

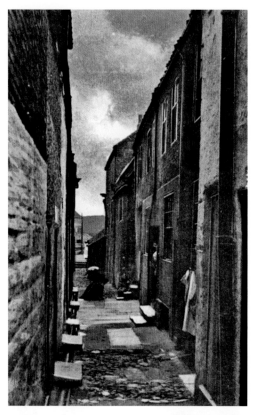

Loggerhead Yard

These views are looking toward Dock End in front of the railway station as it was known before it was filled in to create Langbourne Road and the car park. Concerning the title of the yard, there is a story told of how it acquired the famous piece of woodwork: 'There is in Baxtergate an old fashioned little house which we hope may be long spared the attention of the improvement monger. It is so low that we easily gain a sight of its old roof tiles, its plaster walls and homely windows are suggestive of cosy rooms and warm fireside within. On the wall by the entrance is an image which greatly impresses the stranger. How often have we seen him stop and gaze with admiring eyes upon that work of the carvers' art?

'It seems a French smuggling lugger taken in the early years of the nineteenth century was condemned at Whitby. She was cut into three parts and then sold to Mr Spencelayh, a ship-builder in Larpool woods. The timbers were used for converting a schooner and the figure head was given to Mr Bovil, landlord of the building...This account seems very circumstantial and not unlikely to be true. Nevertheless, it is not in accordance with Whitby pronunciation to change lugger into logger and it is possible that the house itself may at one time have possessed one of the more ancient of public house signs that [consisted of] two silly looking faces with the inscription "We Three Loggerheads Be..." the unsuspecting spectator being, of course, the third.'

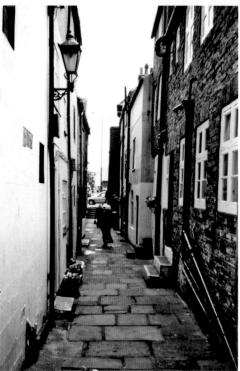

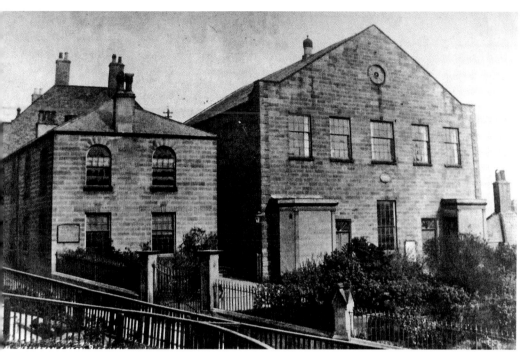

Chapel Yard, Baxtergate

This was sometimes referred to as the Brunswick Chapel Yard and led from Baxtergate where it was a continuation of Beck Yard seen in the bottom photograph. The upper photograph shows the old arrangement of the church and school rooms before they were demolished and rebuilt in 1891–92. The Brunswick Wesleyan Church, up Brunswick Street formerly known as Scate Lane, gave its name to Brunswick Chapel Yard. During the nineteenth century, the name 'Chapel Yard' was the most commonly repeated name of all the yards in Whitby and at one time there were four Chapel Yards.

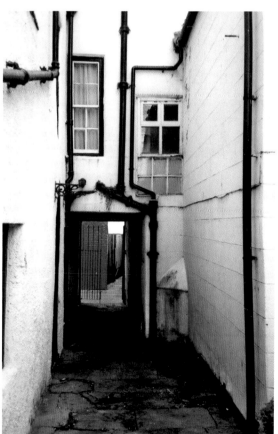

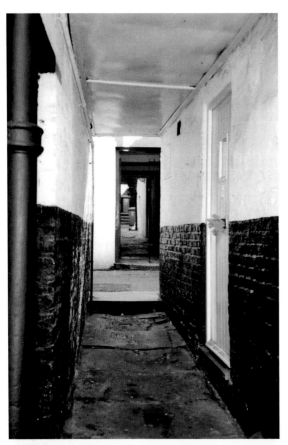

Beck Yard, Baxtergate

In 1909 the MOH wrote, 'Beck's Yard is another of the narrow passages that connect two main streets, in this case, Baxtergate with Station Square; there is want of air space in it, but the houses are well-built and are in good repair'. Here, as we look across Baxtergate, we see Chapel Yard, today locked up preventing through access onto Brunswick Street and Brunswick chapel and Sunday school. Below, a Tom Watson photograph of the Brunswick Rooms attached to Brunswick Church laid out for the tea that was provided to celebrate the opening of the rooms in 1891.

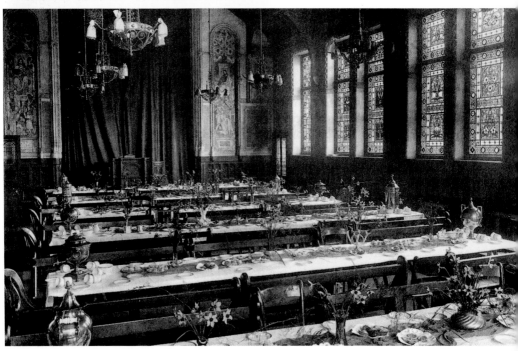

Brunswick Mews, Flowergate

The Revd George Young in his work
A History of Whitby, Vol. II, published
in 1817 wrote 'the streets, being then
without pavement except at the sides,
were worn deep and hollow; and the waste
water, having no drains for its reception,
formed a current in the midst, where it
sometimes stagnated. In the winter season,
the streets, especially at the entrances of
the town, were scarcely passable; but, for
the accommodation of the inhabitants,
some of the principal streets had narrow
walks, paved with flags, in front of the
houses. These walks were most remarkable
. . . the pavement was greatly elevated
above the middle of the street, with steps
descending from one part of the walk to
another, and other steps, at different places,
leading down to the street . . . It was not
until after the year 1750, that our streets
were materially improved, and began
to assume that respectable appearance
which they now wear. Since that time, a
great proportion of the oldest houses have
been rebuilt, or modernised; the thatched
cottages have given place to neat and
commodious dwellings, roofed with tiles.'

Today, Bagdale is the only example of
this type of street with a raised causeway.
At one time you could enter Beck Yard at
Dock End, cross into Chapel Yard, come out
on Brunswick Street and cross and then
climb the steps here in Newton Street and
come out at the top of Flowergate, but now
modern owners with no regard for history
and heritage and new-build housing, have
caused the steps to be bricked up and sadly,
this route is not possible anymore.

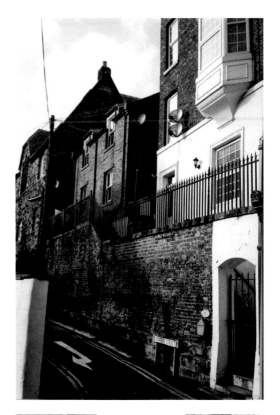

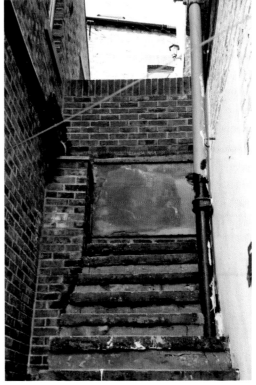

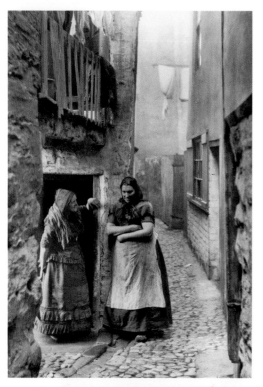

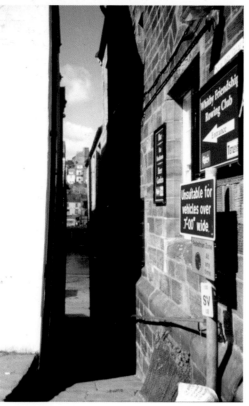

New Way Ghaut, c. 1890

New Way Ghaut, photographed by Sutcliffe, was sometimes known as New Quay Ghaut. In 1817, the Revd George Young, author of *A History of Whitby* in two volumes, suggested that as 'New Way' was nearly one hundred years old, it needed to change its name. It consisted of two lanes, one leading direct from Church Street to the harbourside and the second going toward Tate Hill. This end is now closed up, but it appears to have led to a kiln below Tate Hill and near to the harbour. In 1837, it was described as 'the lane behind the Fox', a public house whose address was given as Kiln Yard. It has been suggested that the Fox, a large inn, was demolished to make way for the erection of the old Cholmley School, built in 1868, which survives as the Fisherman's Club opposite the Church Street post office. The name 'Fox' is actually thought to refer not to an animal, but to a nautical term for two or three strands of rope twisted together. In 1909, the MOH reported it was 'not a very satisfactory place, one reason being that it is paved with cobble stones, so that it is almost impossible to keep it clean as so much dirt and wet settles in the intervals between the stones. The houses are, on the whole, not very bad with the exception of four tenements, which I have advised the Council should be closed, owing to damp and dilapidation. This is under consideration at the end of the year.'

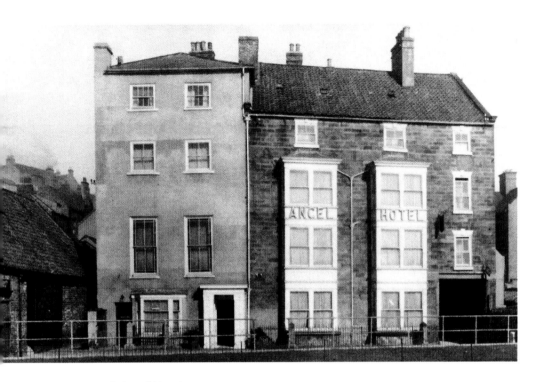

New Quay Road, Angel Hotel

The Angel Hotel was mentioned in 1595 and, by the eighteenth century, it was described as the premier coaching inn; stagecoaches to London and the North first began to run from here in 1795. From 1815–58, the 'Lion Lodge' of Freemasons held their meetings here. It was here also, in 1832, that George Stephenson the railway builder met with the townsfolk of Whitby who invited him to build a railway into this seaport. The hotel was acquired by the Laughton family, of Scarborough, and the nightclub opened in the attached Assembly Room, which was named Laughton's.

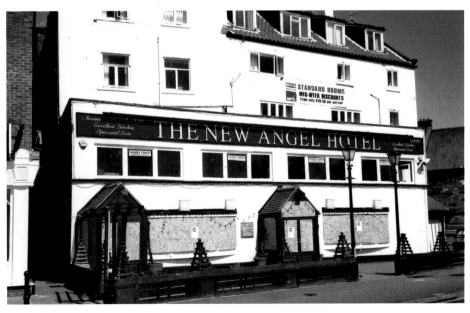

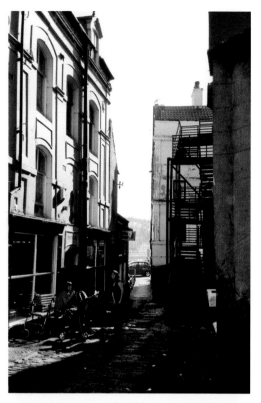

Angel Yard off Baxtergate

Facing onto Baxtergate and the former Talbot Hotel, is Angel Yard, once described as 'sadly non-descript', which is possibly true. Two yards ran up each side of the property from the quayside, which then was only wooden and the width of the present pavement from the waters edge – over the years the Angel Hotel has been completely turned around. The front faced into the yard on Baxtergate and an examination shows that the decorative façade is only confined to this elevation (bottom) – there was no need to waste expense decorating the rear elevation. Known locally as the 'Big A' the hotel underwent a major refurbishment and was renamed in the year 2001 the *New Angel Hotel*. Until recently the building carried two blue plaques, one recalling that in 1832 George Stephenson and the town dignitaries met here to discuss the practicalities of bringing a railway to Whitby; and another commemorates the buildings association with Arthur Machen, the writer and journalist who stayed here during the Second World War when on a journey around the country to report on the conditions of the English people.

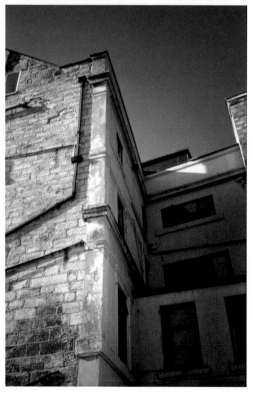

The Assembly Rooms

The top photograph may never be duplicated, certainly not in my lifetime, and was taken when Eves' Garage on the harbour side was demolished. It provides a unique view of part of the old Angel Hotel, behind the Assembly Rooms. This view was quickly obscured by the erection of a block of shops and apartments in 2009. Below, is the New Angel Hotel, undergoing major refurbishment in February 2012, following its closure and sale to new owners in 2011. The Assembly Rooms, first known as St Hilda's Hall, was attached to the Angel Hotel, and had its entrance on Baxtergate. It was erected for public assemblies by Messrs. Weighill, and opened on 19 June 1855 with a grand concert. When first built, the main apartment was 72 feet long, 39 feet broad and 26 feet high, and could accommodate 800 persons; 550 in the body and the remainder in the gallery. This gallery was about 5 feet wide, with balustrades, and was supported by ornamental cantilevers. It was carried along both sides and one end of the hall, the opposite end was occupied by a raised orchestra. Seventeen circular-headed windows admitted light, while the gallery had the same number of sub-lights for ventilation. It was lit by gas issuing from a huge ceiling-hung chandelier and a line of eighteen bronze statuettes holding gas burners in the form of torches, ranged along the walls. At one period, a company of merchants in the town leased it, later it formed part of the Angel Hotel, and is now a nightclub and discothèque.

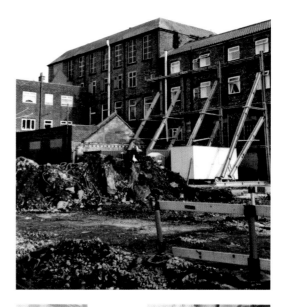

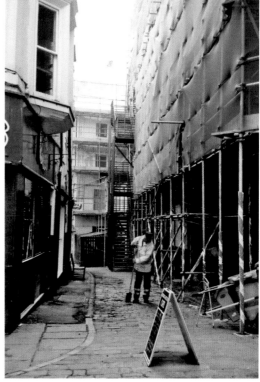

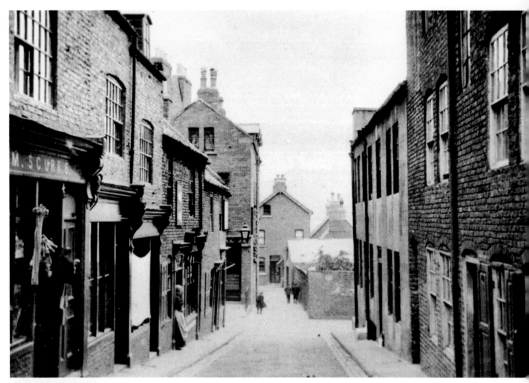

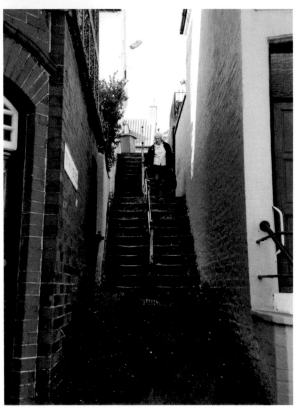

Hunter Street looking toward the Paddock *c.* 1890

The photograph at the bottom shows the Paddock Steps descending into Cliff Street. Whitby's first theatre stood in the Paddock, adjacent to Mr Hunter's house, and is recorded as early as 1763. This was one of the earliest in the country and it stood until 1784. The Paddock was accessed via Cliff Street that formerly ended at a wicket gate, beyond which was a walk along the top of the cliffs until the cutting of the Khyber Pass did away with it, and the end portion of Cliff Street is now known as 'The Mount', and it was here that a school was set up.

Cliff Street & Paddock Steps

Though not as old as many other Whitby Streets, it has some good period houses and was one of the best residential areas. It took its name from the fact that it runs along a cliff edge and was at one time known as 'Wind Lane', from the fact that it was in an exposed position. It may also have had an earlier name of Russell Lane, and lead to Russell Lands, said to have stood above *Hagilsyke* or *Haglelsougate,* the former names for Haggersgate. Two dwelling houses, immediately to the north of Bakehouse Yard, today occupy the site of the old Presbyterian Chapel originally built in 1790. It was remodelled and re-fronted in 1857 in the Gothic style of architecture, after which it could accommodate 450 persons. The Revd George Young, DD, the author of *The History of Whitby* and other works, was minister here from 1806 to 1848 when he died. The interesting looking building at the foot of the Paddock Steps was for many years the dance studio of Miss Millicent Simmonds (1906-97) and her husband Reggie (*d.* 1997). The building was first erected as a studio warehouse for the architect Robert Leonard and carries his initials and date 'R. L. 1888' on the Dutch gable over the door. It has many architectural features including fossil ammonites in the centre of each pebble-dashed concrete panel in the upper levels and fine carving under the various windows. Below, is the distinctive street entrance to 12A Cliff Street.

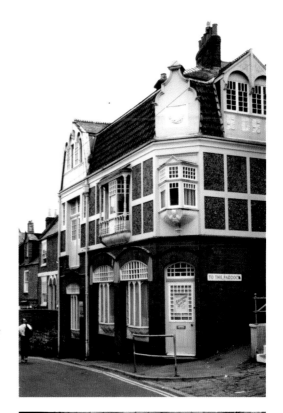

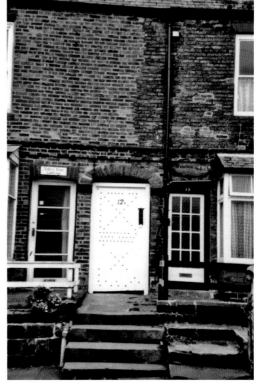

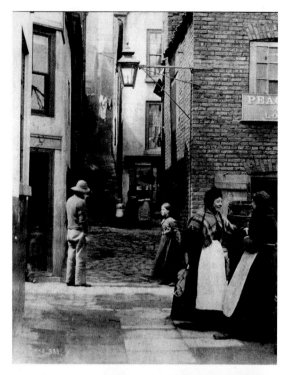

Pier Lane, Haggersgate

Left, the bottom of Pier Lane *c.* 1880 photographed by F. M. Sutcliffe. The extreme left-hand wall in the foreground is the Marine Café once the Marine Hotel. Pier Lane was known as Bath(s) Lane in 1828, taking its title from the Sea Bathing Establishment nearby designed by the Whitby architect John Bolton for the Whitby Public Baths Company, which later became the town's first museum and public library and is today an award winning fish & chip restaurant. At one time, this was the last highway on this side of Whitby and marked the end of the town. In 1909, the MOH reported, 'Pier Lane is well-paved, and only contains two or three houses; these are satisfactory'. Handcarts full of fish were trundled up this steep thoroughfare from the quayside. The Sea Bathing Establishment was erected at a time when sea bathing was in its infancy and for the price of 1s you could hire a tin bath here which would be filled with sea water from the harbour and you sat in it – that's the nearest you got to sea bath at that period. The rules stated that gentlemen must be 'decently attired' in a costume that reached from the 'knee to the neck'. Bathing machines were first introduced during the reign of King George III (1760–1820) to assist swimmers take to the water. In Whitby, the bathing machines were stationed at the bottom of the Khyber Pass and operated by the Argument family during the nineteenth century. Below shows the top of Pier Lane as it comes on to Cliff Street.

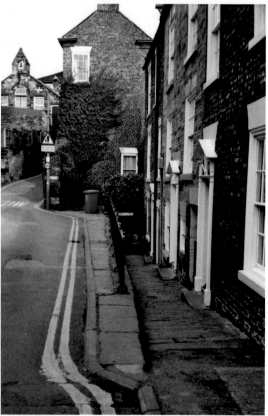

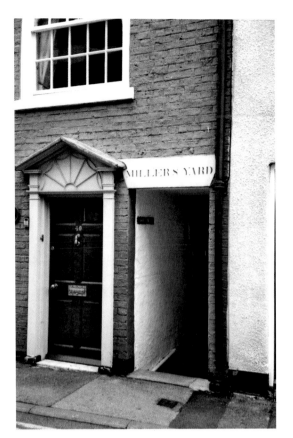

Miller's Yard, Cliff Street

In 1837 a lime house was recorded here with a rateable value of 10s owned by George Miller from whom the yard undoubtedly takes it title. At one period there were three Miller Yards in existence. Miller's Yard on Church Street, mentioned in 1899, was demolished in 1958. Miller's Yard, up Flowergate [1899], was renamed Rose & Crown Yard. The original title came from the shop of W. G. Miller, grocer, in Flowergate. Not far from the entrance to Millers Yard on Cliff Street is was an old sign on a window sill (below).

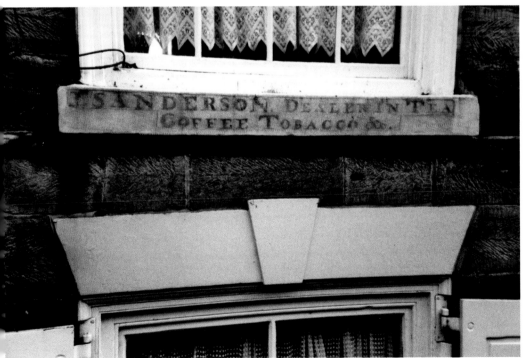

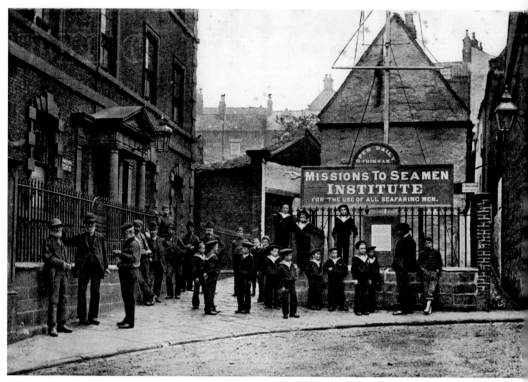

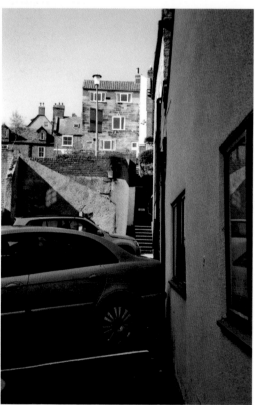

Paradise Yard, Haggersgate

Above, this photograph by F. M. Sutcliffe appeared in a supplement to the *Whitby Gazette* Friday, August 1893 and shows Paradise Yard to the right, with the lamp to light the entrance. It has also been referred to as Arch Yard. In 1899, George Breckon the chimney sweep lived here. In 1909, the MOH recorded it was 'One of the narrow yards, but it is one of the clean ones and is well-kept and contains some nice little houses'. Today it has gone and the area is an open courtyard to Haggersgate House.

Post Office Yard, Baxtergate

For many years the town post office stood on St Anne's Staithe. In 1909, the MOH wrote of this yard, 'There are two stacks of property that were condemned some time ago as being unfit for human habitation, and these have been left to fall into decay'. Later, the post office transferred to a sumptuous building on Baxtergate (above) and the original 'Post Office Yard' became '[Old] Post Office Yard'. Below, a photograph of the staff of the post office taken in the post office yard, off Baxtergate, which can be seen in the background through the entrance arch.

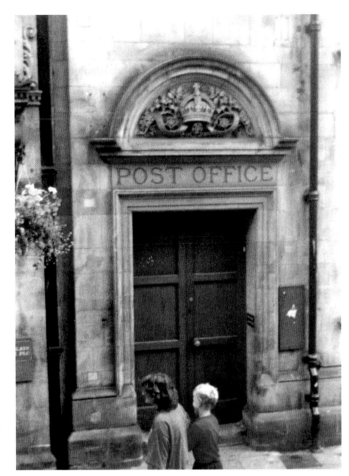

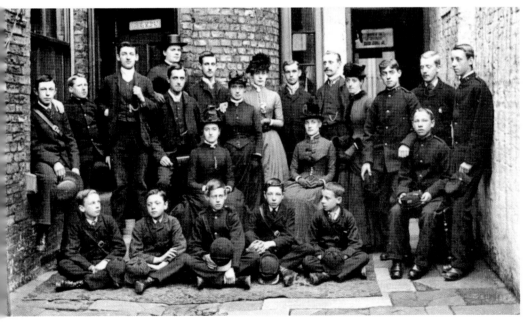

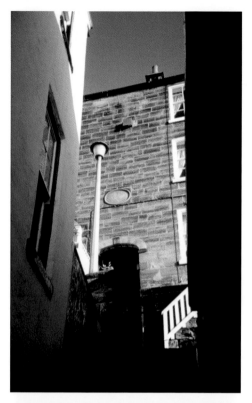

Prospect Place, Church Street

An inscribed stone above the first archway declares, 'Prospect Place Erected by Gideon Smales MDCCCXVI [1816]'. Today, only two rows of houses survive out of three. In 1909, the MOH wrote, 'Prospect Place consists of three rows of well-built stone houses, and is a satisfactory yard in every way. In 1934, it was said to be under the ownership of Annie Readman. Gideon Smales, the builder of Prospect Place, was born 6 March 1766 and died on 11 April 1817; the year after Prospect Place was completed. He was a block and mast maker and a raff merchant. He came from a Quaker family and is interred in the Friends' Burial Ground in Bagdale, although he was 'not in membership' at that time. Smales senior had a son called Gideon born 22 August 1796 who was the eldest surviving son. He was a ship builder and owner and he too is buried in the Quaker Burial ground, although he appears to have abandoned Quakerism and had all his children baptised into the Church of England. Gideon Smales the third, was the son of the above Gideon the second; he died 24 August 1872 of cancer of the throat. Another Gideon Smales was born on 25 October 1817 and baptised on 9 November 1823 at St Mary's parish Church, Whitby as 'Gideon Snares' illegitimate son of Susannah Nares & _____, Whitby, Spinster'. On the marriage certificate to his second wife, dated 1864, at Robin Hood's Bay, his name is Gideon Smales, his occupation given as Wesleyan Minister and his father is declared as Gideon Smales, ship builder.

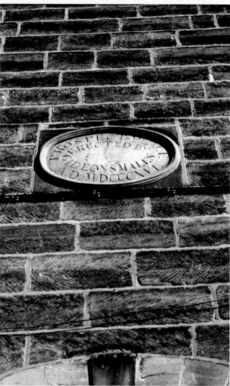

Prospect Place, Church Street

More views of Prospect Place showing the dizzy heights to which it ascends. With access to Church Street it may probably have gone through to The Ropery above. Church Street was first known as 'Kirkgate' in 1318, and originally it was a short street extending from the foot of the 199 Steps to the corner of the market place. Very little of this street was in the town of Whitby proper at that date. Today, the name 'Church Street' applies to the entire distance from the bottom of the 199 Steps to Spital Bridge. Church Street in different sections was known by various names. From the market place to what is today Bridge Street, which then did not exist, was 'High Gate', followed by 'Crossgate' to the end of Grape Lane. Here stood the old tollbooth and this junction still bears the name 'Tatie Market' from the market that grew up around the tollbooth. From that point to Boulby Bank was 'Southgate', and hereabouts the buildings ended. The rest of the roadway to Spital Bridge was merely a track over sand and gravel, and impassable at high water. A gate or turnstile barred the way to all but pedestrians just beyond Boulby Bank, horse traffic traversed Boulby Bank and went by the 'Horse Road' onto the highway, which runs from the abbey to Hawsker and beyond and was an extension of the famously steep and cobbled 'donkey road', the principal road out of Whitby in the medieval period.

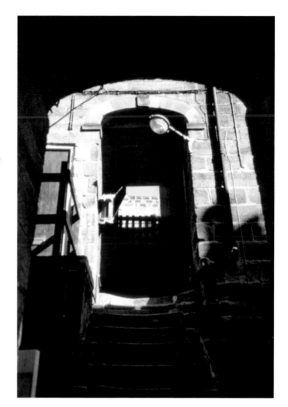

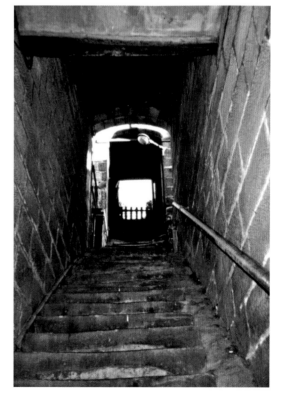

77

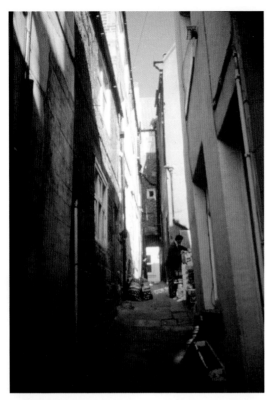

Rose & Crown Yard, Flowergate

Originally this yard was named Miller's
Yard from the shop of W. G. Miller,
grocer, and only took its present title
around 1899. It is known that the present
building, which is today the greengrocer's,
was the property erected by Thomas and
Elizabeth Walker in 1708 as attested by
an inscribed stone down the yard above
an entrance. It was recorded as an inn by
1794 and known as the *Rose & Crown*. In
1909, the MOH wrote that it was
'A satisfactory yard in every way, except I
should like to see the bottom part of this
yard paved'. In 1934, the principal owner
was R. A. Wilson & Son. In 1899, there
were half a dozen jet workers living down
this yard. In 1934, the following persons
lived down the Rose & Crown Yard:
Sydney Stonehouse; William R. Raistrick;
Stephen Boyes; James Stamp; Mary
Readman; William Hill; James Hunter
and James T. White, and they all paid 6s
0d in rates except for James Hunter who
paid a shilling less.

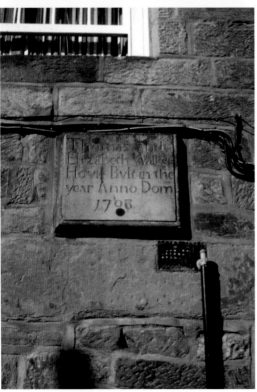

Rose & Crown Yard, Flowergate

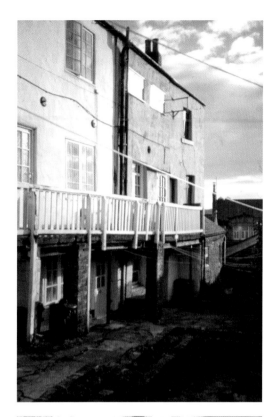

Today, the narrow entrance down a passage opens into a large walled paved yard, and up to recent date was hardly changed with some of the last galleried houses surviving down here with a splendid array of outside privies and the remains of a wash-house. New owners, however, have swept much of the old charm away and have demolished some of the privies. Flowergate is probably the oldest street in Whitby. It was mentioned in the *Domesday Book* as 'Flore' and in 1222, was called 'Floregate'. This was undoubtedly the beginning of the town perimeter, and it is believed that a fortified gatehouse or castle stood at the junction of Flowergate and Brunswick Street on flat land that gave its name to the street (*Flore*, Saxon meaning floor). The site today is covered by the Little Angel public house, which was enlarged following the demolition of Stockton Walk in 1890 by a Mr Winterburn, whose tender for the work was accepted by the Local Board. Stockton Walk was a collection of old houses and shops, together with a raised causeway. Flowergate is now the second principal shopping street in the town. At 4 Flowergate, a stone tablet built into a wall in the cellar bears the initials of Henry Sneaton and the date 1670, and was probably a door lintel moved from the street to here. Henry Sneaton is known to all Yorkshire numismatists as the issuer of a distinctive heart-shaped Trade Token in 1667. He lived in Flowergate until 1707.

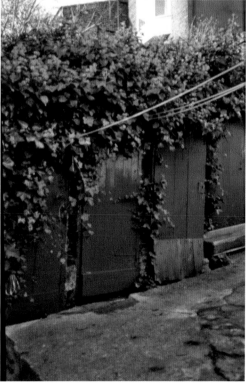

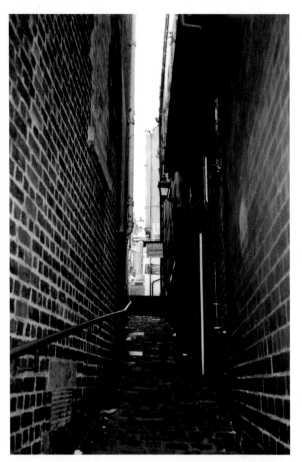

St Anne's Lane, St Anne's Staithe
Formerly known as Helle Lane,
and sometimes Stocking Lane, in
1909 the MOH reported, 'It has, half
way down it, a very nice block of
property, but the rest is very inferior
and at the top there is a stack of
tenement houses which are only just
passable'. This thoroughfare once
descended to the old quay level by
a series of steps leading to a ford
with stepping stones crossing the
harbour to the East Side, to connect
with Ellerby Lane. The entry on the
opposite bank of the harbour can be
seen by a difference in the stonework
beneath an arch. Below, St Anne's
Staithe *c.* 1920.

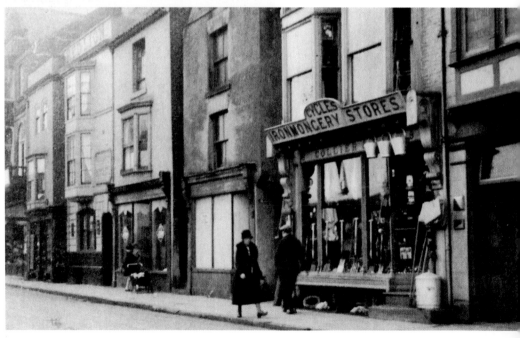

Salt Pan Well Steps

First known as Wood Street from Mr Joseph Wood, it gave access across Church Street or Kirkgate as it was then called to Wood's Quay. However, by 1890, it was commonly referred to as Salt Pan Well Yard, and probably took its name from the short-lived salt business set up by Sir Hugh Cholmley in the seventeenth century in the harbour opposite. In 1909, the MOH reported, 'In Salt Pan Wells the channel is very bad, and the steps are out of repair. At the top there is a stack of fairly good cottages that have been partly rebuilt. Some of the buildings that were used for dwellings are now used for wash-houses or warehouses'. In 1837, the owner of the yard was Thomas Jackson and there were two lime houses here operated by Thomas Clifford who paid 15s 0d in rates. The majority of property, at that date, however, appears to have been classed as 'tenements' and among the residents were Jane Harrison who paid 2s 0d in rates; Susannah Tindall, James Dean, William Gibson and John Smith who all paid 1s 10d in rates. In 1899, the names of the residents included John Hutton, mariner; Daniel Stewart, plater; Robert Mallinson, labourer; John Sayer, carter; and James M. Readman, a joiner. By 1934, it is noticeable that the number of residential properties had increased in number, and thirteen houses were actually numbered.

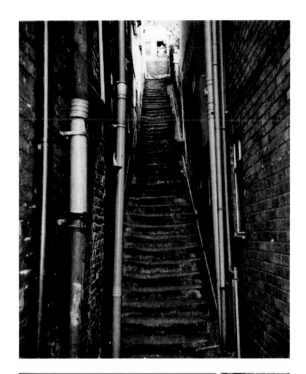

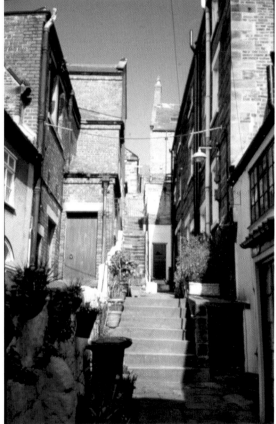

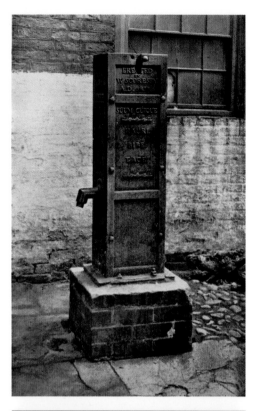

Salt Pan Well Steps, Church Street

At the bottom of Salt Pan Well Steps at one period lived the famous Whitby Whaling Captain William Scoresby, senior (1760–1829), who set up a water pump in 1819 inscribed in Latin – *Suum Cuique. Hauri. Bibe. Tace* – which loosely translated means 'To every one his own, draw, drink [but] be silent'. This was added as an admonishment to the womenfolk who used the pump to 'keep the noise down' while going about their business of drawing water. The pump is now in the town museum. William Scoresby Senior and his son, also named William Scoresby (1789–1857), were two of the most famous and influential whaling captains and inventors of their age. It is said that Capt. Scoresby Senior lived in this yard and he kept a live polar bear chained up in the harbour opposite. Today, this is one of the few yards (or more correctly, steps) that are accessible to the public and well-worth the effort to climb to the Ropery (and then back along this road toward the town, descending by the new way, Caedmon's Trod, into Greens Yard and Church Street). Near the top, on the Ropery, is a timber-framed cruck building dated 1594, one of the last of its type in the town and clearly showing its timber construction as it has been reduced in size and the end gable was once an internal wall.

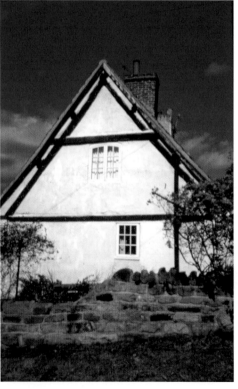

Staffordshire Place, Flowergate

The upper yard along the side of Staffordshire House was formerly known as Old Gas Office Yard. The Flowergate façade of nineteenth-century white-brick belies the age of the buildings behind, one of which bears the date and initials 'R. M. B. 1736'. In 1909, the MOH wrote of the yard, 'Quite satisfactory, no fault can be found'. The same can be said of the yard today. The large elaborate Victorian sign board above the second floor windows still survives to this day in exactly the same position. The residents of many of Whitby yards are quite proud of there properties, and when I often took people on town walks up and down the yards, the two elderly ladies of Dolphin Cottage and Georgian Cottage would come out and talk with the group about life in the yards and how it has changed over the years – and sometimes if it was a small group they would provide a welcome 'cuppa'. Edwin Todd was a high end emporium supplying quality merchandise for the middle class residents of the town and visitors to Whitby who might like to take home a souvenir. The last of this type of shop, Horne's on Skinner Street, closed in 2011, but the clock on its bracket high on the wall facing along Skinner Street for all to see, still remains. Uncannily, the day old Mr Horne died, the clock was damaged at the precise hour and stopped! It was only later repaired.

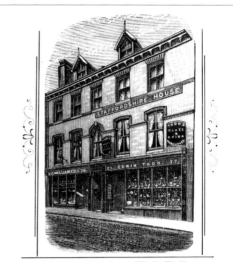

EDWIN ÷ TODD,
GLASS & CHINA DEALER,
Staffordshire House, Flowergate, Whitby.

The Stock comprises Goods from all the Best Manufacturers.
Sole Agent in Whitby for Doulton's Ware, Royal Worcester Ware, Goss' China, and the Coal Port China Company.

Fig. 14 A 19th century advertisement for Staffordshire House.

60

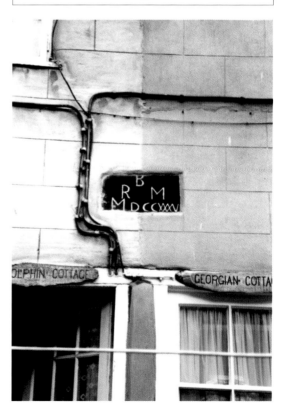

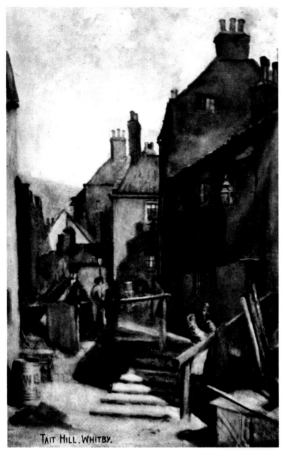

TAIT HILL. WHITBY.

Tait Hill off Church Street

This area of Whitby known as Tait [Tate] Hill was a densely populated part of the town, but when it began to deteriorate, it became known as the 'Rookery' where even larger numbers of poor people crammed into the housing. In 1899, the Steam Dye Works of James Thompson could also be found here. In 1909, the MOH wrote, 'Now generally kept clean, the condition of the paving is satisfactory except where there are cobble stones in the far corner, and these have required repair for some time'. Much of the dilapidated property was demolished in the 1960s and the foundation of buildings can be seen on Sandside off Tait Hill.

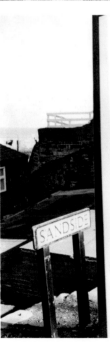

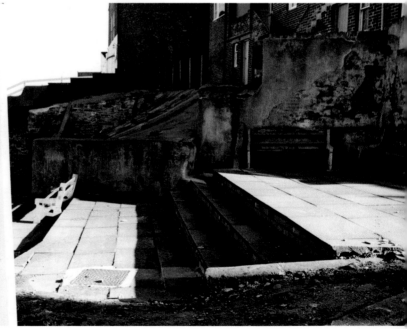

SANDSIDE

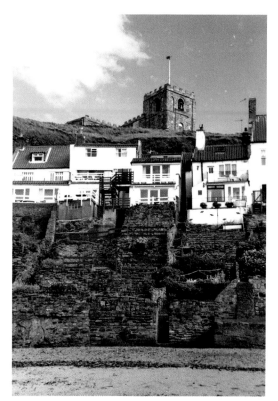

Tait Hill from the Beach

Much of Tate Hill has been lost to the sea, pushed down into the waters by successive landslides from the unstable cliffs above and, from the sands, it is easy to spot the foundations of houses that came all the way down to the beach. In not so ancient times, the beach at low tide was used as a 'drying ground' by the women, to dry their washing on, by simply placing the clothes on the fine sand. It was on Tate Hill sands that the ship which featured in Bram Stoker's famous Gothic novel *Dracula* ran aground.

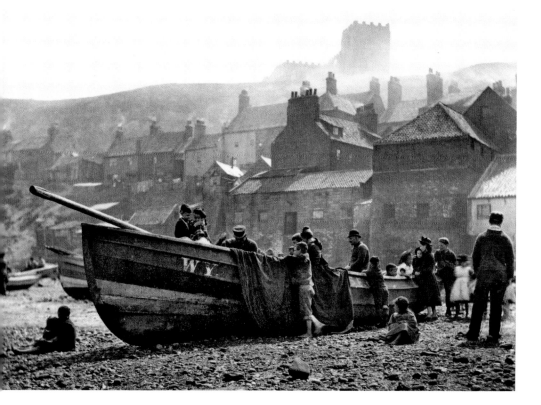

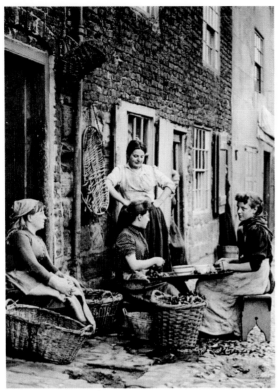

Tait Hill, Unknown Yard

Girls 'skaning' [opening] mussels; a photograph taken by Frank Sutcliffe in the 1890s, in a yard off Tait Hill. This task was performed by the womenfolk, ready for baiting the fishermen's long lines. The collecting, skaning and baiting of mussels were regular and major preoccupations of fishermen's families. As local supplies dwindled, mussels were often brought from Boston or even the West Coast. Hanging from the wall can be seen a flat wicker 'skep' used for carrying the coiled long line with its wicked barbed hooks. Below, a view of Tait Hill in 1945, by the famous Cleveland artist Alec Wright.

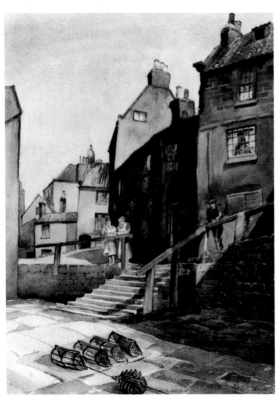

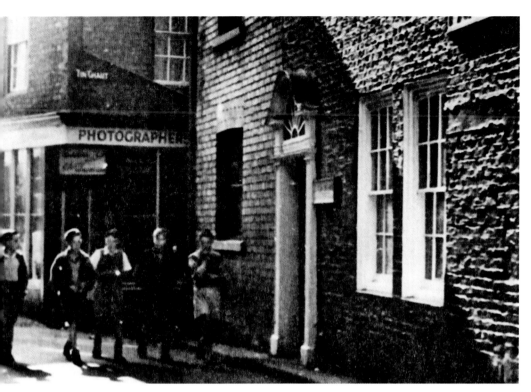

Tin Ghaut

Above, the entrance to Tin Ghaut in 1913, standing next to the house in which Capt. James Cook lived and which is today the Capt. Cook Museum, before demolition. The photographer's shop was once the 'Britannia Inn' from which it is said the ghaut took its name in the local dialect – 't'inn Ghaut'. Some say that the word ghaut is from the Norse meaning a narrow passage leading to a river. The house that is now the Captain Cook Museum was built for John and Susannah Dring in 1724 and in Cook's day was owned by Walker.

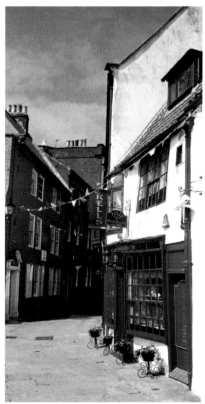

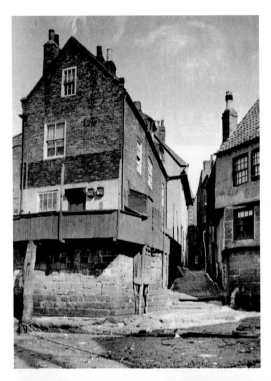

Ghaut, The Word

It is not known how the word 'ghaut' came into use in Whitby when apparently it is not used anywhere else in the country. The *Oxford English Dictionary* (*OED*) states that the word is derived from the Hindi '*ghat*', and that it was first used as an Anglo-Indian phrase in 1603 when Europeans named a range of mountains in India, 'The Ghauts'. Later, in 1698, it was used to describe a mountain pass or defile, and from this came to mean 'a narrow passage'. It is not difficult to understand its application in 1783 to describe 'a passage or steps, leading down to a river'. A second definition in the *OED* states 'a landing place of a ford or ferry', both it will be noted, relating to a river. The Revd Young writing of the word ghaut or gaut suggests it might simply be a contraction of the phrase 'go out', mentioning beforehand that in this context 'on both sides of the harbour there are openings, at various places to admit a passage to the ships'. The spelling of the word lends itself to a common mispronunciation rhyming with 'caught'. Listening to local dialect reveals, however, that it rhymes with 'goat'. In James Halliwell's *Dictionary of Archaic and Provincial Words* (3rd Edition, 1855) the word 'goat' appears, defined as 'stepping stones', which relates closely to both a river and 'the place of a ford'.

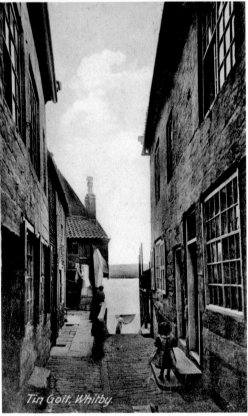

Tin Goit, Whitby.

T'inn Ghaut

This yard took its name from the Britannia Inn that marked its entrance, which stood near to what is today the Captain Cook Museum. However, that old alley was formerly called 'Rudgate' and was one of the landing places for ships moored above the bridge when the upper harbour was full. The area here was demolished during the 1960s and the site of Tin Ghaut is now a car park. Originally, however, Tin Ghaut stood at the other end of Grape Lane, where a gap beside the Dolphin Hotel marks the site of the Raffled Anchor Inn, beside which the ghaut down to the harbour was first named Tin Ghaut. Before then, it was known as Rippon's Ghaut. In 1899, Tin Ghaut was occupied by William Whittup, labourer; George Griffin, riveter; Charles Clarke, labourer; Arthur Hunter, carpenter; John Corter, blacksmith; Mrs Jane Garnisway; Joseph House, labourer; William Bennet; William Akeroyd, iron-monger's porter; M. Storry, labourer; Mrs Ann Elder, and C. Howard, brewer's assistant. In 1934, the ghaut had property numbers that had increased with two properties being sub-divided. No. 5 became 5 and 5A and No. 11 became 11 and 11A in which the latter property resided Sarah Elizabeth Laking and it was owned by John William Ollet who is given as living at No. 10 and No. 11. The majority of the housing was rated at 4s 0d but No. 11 was only rated at 2s 0d, which suggests that this may have been an outbuilding or a semi-derelict slum tenement.

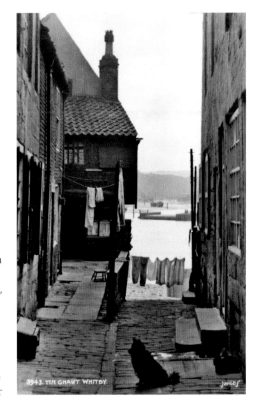

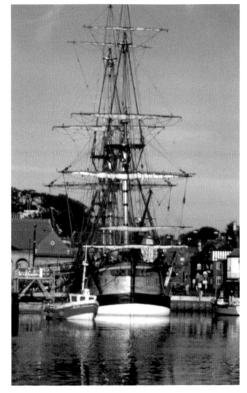

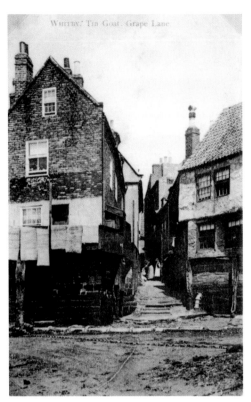

Tin Ghaut From the Harbour (Low Tide)

It was common place for women to hang washing over the balcony, as can be seen in the top photograph looking into Tin Ghaut from the harbour. Often these balconies were perilous constructions, and possibly homemade as in the lower photograph, which shows clearly the balcony in both views, supported on what appears to be a tree trunk. The property to the right is undoubtedly an earlier medieval timber-framed jettied house and separated Tin Ghaut from Alder Waste Ghaut, which was the adjacent yard. All of this area was cleared in the 1950s and 1960s.

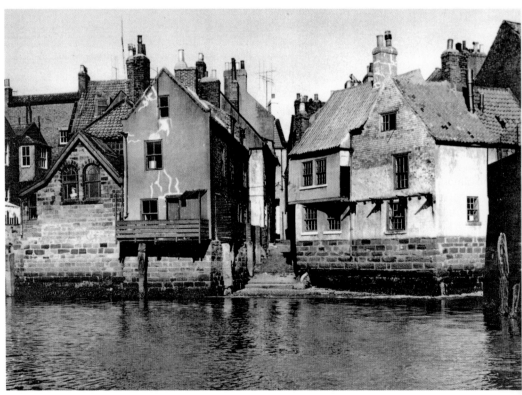

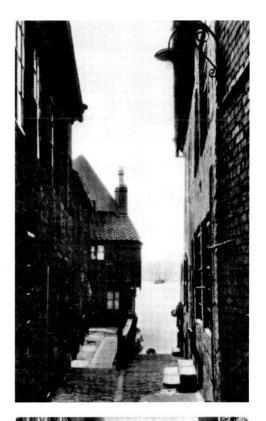

Tin Ghaut Towards the Harbour

Because of adverse geographic factors, Whitby never quite achieved the status of a major port. The surrounding region was never densely populated, and communications with its hinterland have usually been sketchy. The river Esk, until the railway of 1865, offered no useful route through its valley. Consequently, what importance the port formerly possessed was strictly related to the sea rather than to its hinterland. Efforts were sometimes made to remedy this situation, but without success. A canal was projected during the 'canal mania' year of 1793 to link the town with Pickering, but the expense of the undertaking and the slender chances of much return on it caused the plan to be dropped. The sea, on the other hand, brought Whitby a fair measure of business until the start of the twentieth century. The harbour was often a necessary port of call for sailing colliers damaged or sheltering from a storm. As many as fifty vessels are known to have sought refuge there in one day when exceptionally poor weather threatened the coal fleet. The town was well-placed to participate in the great Arctic whale fishery, and its position was protected enough to encourage shipbuilding on a moderate scale, both fulfilling naval contracts and constructing local vessels Trade was mainly coastal in character and can almost be dismissed as coal 'in' and alum 'out'. At various times, the shipment of whale oil and bone, and dried fish and sailcloth, was also important. Timber from the Baltic (and occasionally Canada), iron, hemp, and wheat were among the lesser imports.

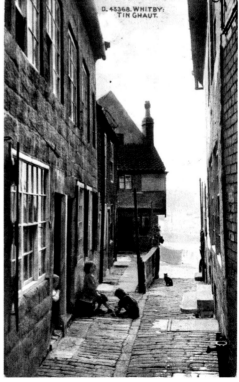

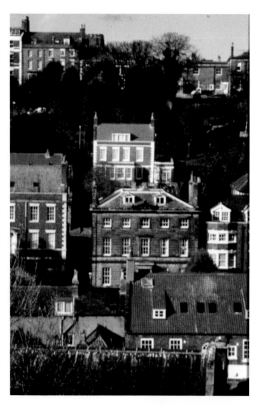

Union Road off Bagdale

Although designated a road, it is in reality a series of steep stone steps rising up to St Hilda's Terrace, where it continues alongside Stone House to end on the street known as the Back of St Hilda's Terrace (from which by way of Stonehouse Gardens, there is a way through to Well Close Square). At one period, at the foot of Union Road on Bagdale, a horse trough and pump stood. Beside the steps in the lower length of Union Road runs a steep cobbled way. Stone House, which can just be seen at the top right with the tall chimney, was the residence of William Stonehouse (1817-98) who was born at Commondale. After an apprenticeship to a painter at Guisborough, and short periods of employment as a journeyman at Malton and in London, he came to Whitby in 1844 and started business as a painter and decorator in Church Street. In 1848, after establishing a successful photographic studio in Church Street, which was later transferred to the Pier, he gave up the business of painter and decorator. At the time of his death he was President of the Whitby Subscription Library. He was also keenly interested in the Whitby Institute, of which he was, at its last meeting, the sole surviving founder. An avid collector, William Stonehouse died in February 1898, and left to the Literary & Philosophical Society his entire collection of books printed in Whitby, or relating to the town and neighbourhood, together with a legacy of £100.

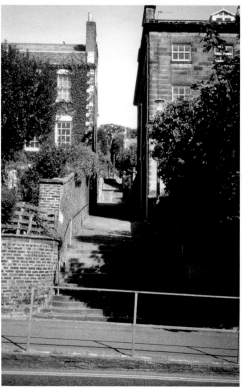

Waterloo Yard, Flowergate

It was down Waterloo Yard off Flowergate that Frank Meadow Sutcliffe (1853–1941) the famous nineteenth-century photographer had an early studio. Frank M. Sutcliffe was the eldest son of Thomas Sutcliffe, a watercolour artist, etcher, and lithographer, of Leeds, where Frank was born in October 1853. Following a period as a clerk after leaving school, he took up an interest in photography, still then in its infancy, to which his father encouraged him. In 1871, after numerous holidays to Whitby, the Sutcliffe family moved here to live at Ewe Cote Hall. Unfortunately, within twelve months of arriving, his father was tragically killed. Frank Sutcliffe began his photographic career from this date. Marrying a Whitby post office clerk, Eliza Duck, they moved to Tunbridge Wells with the idea of becoming a photographer but soon returned to Whitby with their child who was born there. He set up his first studio in a vacant jet shop in Waterloo Yard, but later moved after quickly establishing a reputation for producing the then fashionable *cartes-de-visite*. Around 1890, the Star Theatre was down this yard, which later became the Waterloo Cinema in 1910 in what had become by that date Waterloo Hall. This closed for a period and reopened as the Ritz Cinema before finally closing its doors in the 1980s. For a time it stood empty once more and was used intermittently as an indoor market before being demolished when residential property was erected on the site in 2001. Today, the yard is hardly recognisable. Top: entrance to Waterloo Place on extreme left of A. E. Hanson's outfitters.

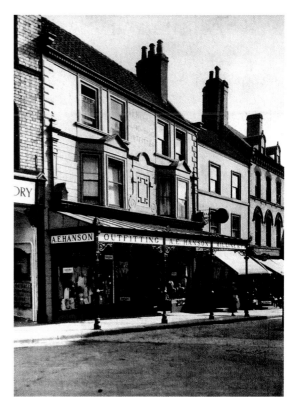

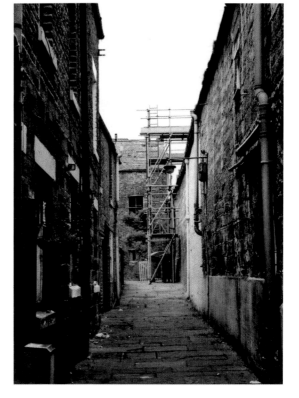

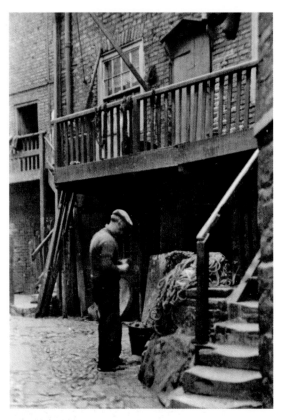

Wilson's Yard

In 1909, the MOH wrote 'Wilson's Yard is satisfactory, so far as I can see, although a cobble stone nuisance exists and the houses are not of the best, but are kept clean'. Both the fisherman mending his nets and the woman below are using the public bakehouse oven as a 'table'. In 1934, the yard was mostly residential with no businesses recorded. Among the residents were Thomas Hutchinson, Richard Hansell Junior, Mary Ann Hansell, Isabell Elder and Bertie Linsley; but the majority of property appears to have been owned by A. E. Hoggarth. In the medieval period and after, with the introduction of the Hearth Tax etc, many poorer households could not afford fires and fireplaces, which often incorporated an oven for baking. Because of this factor, there sprang up the communal bakehouse to provide baking facilities, whereby dough mixed and homemade pies could be sent, and for a small price the baker would bake the article. In large towns, the Public Bakehouse was an important institution. In Whitby, six public bakehouses alone existed on the East Side, including one at the rear of No. 7 Sandgate which was underneath a shop and opened onto the harbour. On West Side, Bakehouse Yard, connecting Haggersgate and Cliff Street, was the site of another. It is known that the bakehouse existed prior to 1654 and was associated with Bakehouse Garth, a plot of land adjacent. In 1817, the bakehouse was in the ownership of Henry Sutherland.

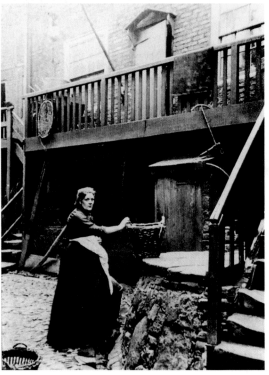

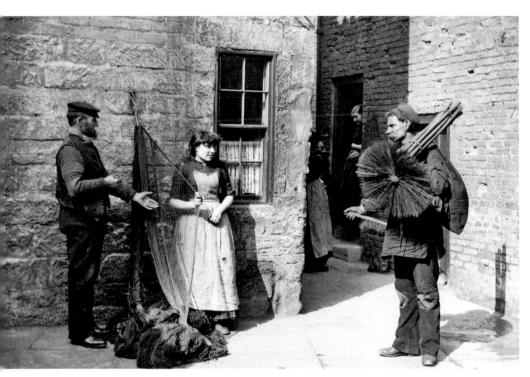

Unknown Yard, Whitby

An unknown yard showing a fisherman and daughter/wife mending a net while chatting with the local sweep William Batchelor; this is detail from a photograph by Sutcliffe and is no doubt carefully posed. Nevertheless, it is an evocative image of the people who lived in these numerous yards and alleys in Whitby. Women gossiped and men passed the time of day as they went about their daily business. It is interesting to note the two types of building construction sat side by side – brick and stone, no doubt quarried locally at Aislaby or on the Abbey Cliff.

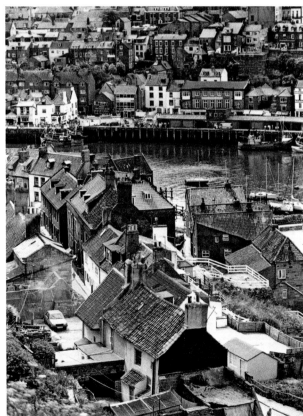

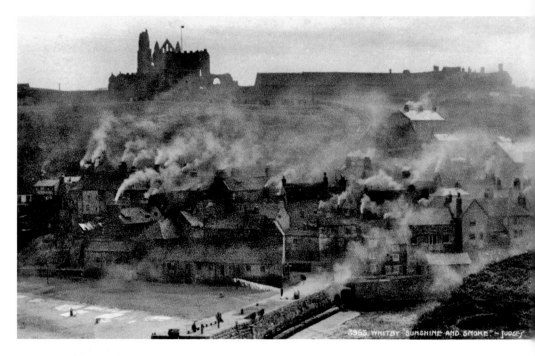

Sunshine and Smoke, Whitby

Two contrasting images of Whitby from West Cliff, looking toward the east side, showing Mary Linskill's 'haven under the hill' dominated by the church and abbey. The legacy of the pollution of previous centuries can be found in the smoke-blackened graves in St Mary's churchyard, and down some of the yards and narrow thorough-fares you can find grime encrusted brickwork. Today, Whitby plays a major part in the tourist industry of the North, its attraction being the old buildings and streets of past times – people thrive on nostalgia, and here in the yards of Whitby there is a wealth of history to be found.

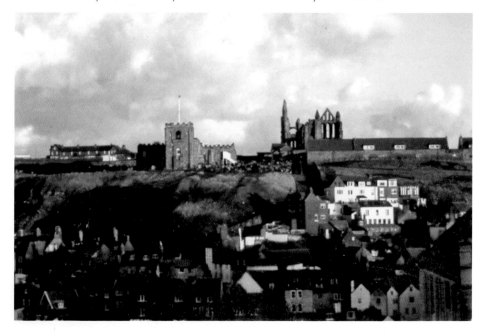